P9-EAO-002

WORLD WAR II:

THE PACIFIC

Sean Sheehan

WORLD ALMANAC® LIBRARY

Please visit our web site at: www.worldalmanaclibrary.com
For a free color catalog describing World Almanac® Library's list of high-quality books
and multimedia programs, call 1-800-848-2928 (USA) or 1-800-387-3178 (Canada).
World Almanac® Library's fax: (414) 332-3567.

Library of Congress Cataloging-in-Publication Data

Sheehan, Sean, 1951-
    World War II: The Pacific / by Sean Sheehan.
        p. cm. — (Atlas of conflicts)
    Includes bibliographical references and index.
    ISBN 0-8368-5670-8 (lib. bdg.)
    ISBN 0-8368-5677-5 (softcover)
    1. World War, 1939-1945—Campaigns—Pacific Area—Juvenile literature. [1. World War, 1939-1945—
Campaigns—Pacific Area—Maps for children.] I. Title. II. Series.
    D767.S5296 2004
    940.54'26—dc22
                                                     2004045159

This North American edition first published in 2005 by
World Almanac® Library
330 West Olive Street, Suite 100
Milwaukee, WI 53212 USA

Produced by Arcturus Publishing Limited.
Series concept: Alex Woolf
Editor: Philip de Ste. Croix
Designer: Simon Burrough
Cartography: The Map Studio
Consultant: Paul Cornish, Imperial War Museum, London
Picture researcher: Thomas Mitchell

World Almanac® Library editor: Gini Holland
World Almanac® Library design: Steve Schraenkler
World Almanac® Library production: Jessica Morris

All the photographs in this book, except for that appearing on page 41, were supplied by Getty Images
and are reproduced here with permission. The photograph on page 41 was taken by Joe Rosenthal
and is reproduced courtesy of Popperfoto.

Editor's Note:
In Japanese and Chinese, family names are placed first, but they are used in this book as given names—
as they were by the West during World War II. The exception is Mao Zedong, who continued as a leader
until his death in 1976, and became internationally known, with correct reference to his family name,
as Chairman Mao.

Printed in Italy

1 2 3 4 5 6 7 8 9 08 07 06 05 04

CONTENTS

CHAPTER 1
JAPANESE VICTORIES

Japanese troops parade through the Chinese city of Shanghai, which they captured in November 1937 after more than four months of fighting.

After many centuries of isolation from most of the world, Japan was well on its way to becoming a modern country by the 1930s. With seventy million people to feed, Japan welcomed Western technology but lacked natural resources, such as oil and rubber, which were vital for a modernizing country. Unlike nations such as Britain and France, Japan also lacked an overseas empire in Asia that could provide it with wealth and natural resources. To remedy this, Japan took aggressive action to occupy Manchuria (a region in northern China) in 1931. Six years later, Japan extended its control by going to war with China. This 1937 invasion of China, however, did not lead to a complete victory there.

When World War II started in 1939, it was at first a European war that mainly involved Germany fighting other western European nations. This outbreak of war in Europe encouraged Japanese leaders who saw fur-

A WAR ECONOMY

During the 1930s, governments in Japan spent more and more on their military buildup. These statistics show Japan developing a war economy.

Military budget as percentage of total government spending:
1931 29 percent
1932 38 percent
1933 39 percent
1934 44 percent
1935 47 percent
1936 48 percent
1937 72 percent
1938 75 percent
1939 72 percent
1940 66 percent
—From *The Oxford Companion to World War II*, edited by I.C.B. Dear

ther military expansion as the only way to make their country rich. By 1941, France and the Netherlands had been defeated by Germany, and Britain seemed reluctant to interfere. Japan seized this opportunity to take over the Asian colonies of these weakened European powers. The natural resources of these colonies would enable Japan to defeat China, build up its own empire, and stop relying on imports from hostile foreign countries like the United States.

THE UNITED STATES

The United States was the major stumbling block to Japan's ambitions. Although only the Philippines and a few islands in the Pacific were under U.S. control, the United States had its own ambitions in the region. The United States particularly wanted to influence events in China, and had

no intention of sharing naval power in the Pacific with Japan. In 1941, Japan began to run out of essential imports after the United States restricted its trade. This economic war got more bitter when Japan moved into southern French Indochina (now Cambodia, Laos, and Vietnam). The United States and Britain froze all their Japanese funds and cut essential oil supplies to Japan.

Japan either had to back down, by withdrawing from Manchuria, China, and French Indochina, or seize control of both the European colonies in Asia and their natural resources. This would bring armed conflict with the U.S., but one way of dealing with this threat would be to launch a surprise attack on the U.S. Navy and destroy its Pacific fleet.

Admiral Isoroku Yamamoto, the Commander in Chief of the Japanese Navy, planned a surprise attack

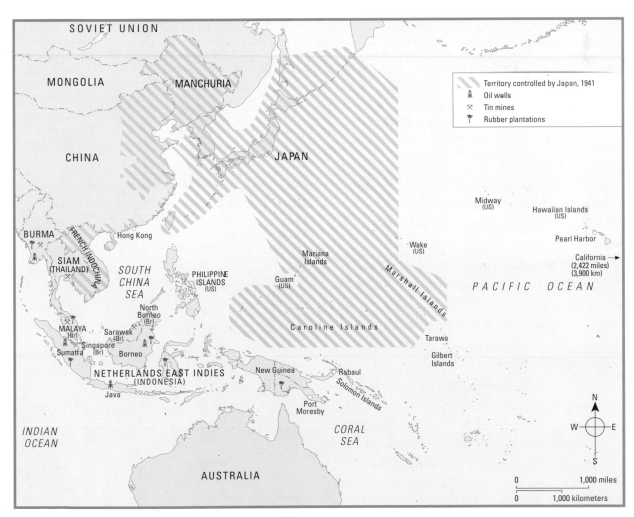

Japan, Britain, France, the Netherlands, and the United States held possessions with key natural resources in the Southwest Pacific before war broke out in December 1941.

on Hawaii that was meant to destroy the U.S. fleet that had been stationed there since the previous year. In late November 1941, Yamamoto sent the code "Climb Mount Niitaka" for six Japanese aircraft carriers to set sail from the northeast of Japan and travel some 4,039 miles (6,500 km) to Hawaii, maintaining radio silence to avoid detection.

On December 7, early in the morning, 183 Japanese planes gathered in a V-formation after taking off from the six aircraft carriers positioned north of Hawaii. It took them more than an hour to reach the island of Oahu, guided to their target by music from a local radio station. Shortly before 8 A.M., bombs began to rain down on the island's harbor and airfields. A second wave of attackers arrived at 8:40 A.M. and inflicted more damage. U.S. losses totaled eighteen sunk or badly damaged ships, including six battleships, 162 aircraft, and the lives of 2,403 servicemen and civilians. The Japanese lost twenty-nine planes and their crews.

U.S. naval power was not destroyed, however, mainly because the three aircraft carriers based at Hawaii were all out at sea at the time of the attack. A third Japanese attack, targeting the harbor's fuel tanks and repair facilities, was called off for fear of a counterattack from the aircraft carriers. If the fuel dumps had been destroyed, Pearl Harbor would have been permanently put out of action.

The United States and Japan were now at war. Various claims have been made that advance warning of the attack was kept secret by U.S. President Franklin D. Roosevelt and by Winston Churchill, Britain's wartime leader, because they wanted the United States to go to war. Historians have found no convincing evidence for this. There were intelligence reports that had indicated that something was to happen in December, but no one put them together and drew the conclusion

that Pearl Harbor was in danger of attack.

Unlike the U.S. fleet in Pearl Harbor, the British were expecting the Japanese to attack Malaya

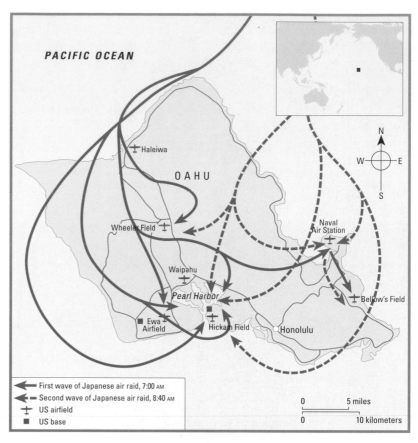

Above: The Japanese bombing of Pearl Harbor was a complete surprise because no one expected a long-distance attack from the north.

EYE WITNESSES

Leonard J. Fox, writing a letter home on board the U.S.S. *Helena* at the time, remembers what he saw on the ground: *"Torpedo planes swooped in from almost over my head and started toward 'Battleship Row' dropping their lethal fish [torpedos]. First the* Oklahoma *. . . then it was the* West Virginia *taking blows in her innards . . . and now it is the* Arizona *. . . Men were swimming for their lives in the fire-covered waters of Pearl Harbor."*
—From *The Pacific Campaign*, Dan Van Der Vat

U.S. warships in Pearl
Harbor proved an easy
target because few of
their guns were manned
and the ammunition was
locked away.

Left: Japanese forces gather at the southern tip of the Malayan peninsula.

Below: The Japanese attack on Malaya, planned to begin at exactly the same time as the attack on Pearl Harbor on December 7, 1941, accidentally began a short while earlier. Siam was also attacked.

(now W. Malaysia). They knew the Japanese would probably land on the beaches in the border area around north Malaya and south Siam (now Thailand). That is exactly what happened shortly after midnight on December 8, 1941. Local time in Hawaii was then 6 A.M. on December 7. It would be almost two hours before the first wave of planes reached Pearl Harbor, so the landings in south Siam and Malaya were Japan's first aggressive action in the Pacific war.

THE INVASION OF
MALAYA
Waiting for the Japanese was a large army of British-led troops, composed mostly of Indians and some Australians. Although outnumbered, the Japanese forces advanced at a blistering pace down the peninsula towards Singapore.

Most of the Japanese forces had no previous experience of jungle warfare but they were battled-hardened from fighting in China. Many of the troops they were fighting were inexperienced, and some of the Indian troops had never seen a tank before they faced

some of the eighty transported by the Japanese. The Japanese also brought bicycles to travel down the well-maintained roads, and they used maps copied from

Map

SIAM (THAILAND)

☐ Bangkok

FRENCH INDOCHINA (LAOS, CAMBODIA, VIETNAM)

☐ Saigon

8 Dec 1941

8 Dec 1941: 28 transports and escorts rendezvous.

8 Dec 1941

8 Dec 1941

8 Dec 1941
☐ Kota Bharu

SOUTH CHINA SEA

Penang ○
22 Dec 1941

MALAYA (MALAYSIA)

10 Dec 1941: *Repulse & Prince of Wales* sunk.

31 Dec 1941
☐ Kuantan

13 Jan 1942 ☐ Kuala Lumpur

SUMATRA

31 Jan 1942 ○ Johore Bahru
Singapore

→ Japanese landings and advance
←- British retreat
↓ Japanese aircraft attack Royal Navy

0   100 miles
0   200 kilometers

school atlases. When faced with enemy resistance, one Japanese tactic was to go around the obstacle through the jungle or to use boats to bypass it along the coastline. The Japanese were also able to attack from the air, flying in from Indochina (now Cambodia, Laos, and Vietnam) and attacking British airfields. They quickly gained control of the skies over Malaya.

The defenders were not prepared for the well-trained and experienced Japanese who easily brushed aside attempts to hold them back. In only ten weeks, the Japanese had reached the southern tip of the peninsula. At this point, only a narrow stretch of water divided the mainland from the island of Singapore, where the retreating Allied soldiers were now concentrated for a final battle with their enemy.

The islands of the Philippines—which served as a U.S. military base in Asia—were around 6,835 miles (11,000 km) from the U.S. West Coast and 4,971 miles (8,000 km) from Pearl Harbor, but only 1,243 miles (2,000 km) from Japan. General Douglas MacArthur,

LOSS OF BATTLESHIPS

Two British battleships, HMS *Prince of Wales* and HMS *Repulse*, were dispatched from Singapore to intercept Japanese invasion forces. They were sunk off Malaya's east coast on December 10, 1941 in a land-based air attack; 840 men lost their lives. War correspondent O.D. Gallagher was on the *Repulse* "*. . . They were bombers. Flying straight at us. All our guns pour high-explosives at them, including shells so delicately fused that they explode if they merely graze cloth fabric. But they swing away, carrying out a high-powered evasive action without dropping anything at all. I realise now what the purpose of the action was. It was a diversion to occupy all our guns and observers on the air defence platform at the summit of the main mast. There is a heavy explosion and the Repulse rocks.*"

—From the *Daily Express*, December 12, 1941

Before 1941, few thought that battle cruisers like HMS *Repulse* could be sunk from the air.

Above: The controversial General Douglas MacArthur was admired as well as criticized by historians.

Right: Unlike Pearl Harbor, an attack on the Philippines was anticipated, but U.S. forces were still defeated.

Below: Japanese General Masaharu Homma sets foot on Philippine soil to oversee the capture of the islands.

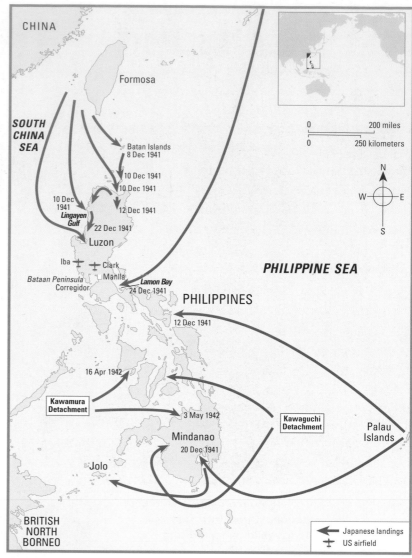

military commander of U.S. forces in the Philippines, argued that the islands could be defended. He built up a force of 30,000 U.S. troops and more than 100,000 Filipinos. The Philippines had the largest concentration of U.S. air power in the Pacific, with B-17 bombers and more than one hundred P-40 fighter aircraft.

Over nine hours passed between news of Pearl Harbor first reaching MacArthur's headquarters and the arrival of Japanese attack planes over Luzon. Some historians question why nothing was done during this period, and why B-17s and P-40s were still on the ground at Clark airfield for the Japaneses to attack and destroy. The Japanese also surprised and wiped out a squadron of U.S. aircraft then returning from a patrol.

Japanese soldiers celebrate the capture of a large American gun on Bataan; it took three months before they were finally able to capture the peninsula, early in April 1942.

MacArthur had lost half of his aircraft on the same day (December 8, 1941) that Japanese troops began landing on the Batan Islands north of Luzon.

Smaller landings took place over the next few days, but the main Japanese invasion force arrived on December 22 in Lingayen Gulf on the west of Luzon. Two days later, more Japanese landed on the east coast in Lamon Bay and it became clear that General Masaharu Homma, commanding the Japanese, hoped to trap the defending forces in a pincer movement. MacArthur realized this and decided to withdraw from around the capital city of Manila. Troops were ordered to retreat to the Bataan peninsula while the military command and the Philippine government withdrew to the island of Corregidor, south of the peninsula.

BOMBING MANILA

Carlos Romulo was working in Manila on December 8 when Japanese planes suddenly appeared in the sky: *"Fifty-four Japanese sky monsters, flashing silver in the bright noonday, were flying in two magnificently formed Vs. Above the scream of the sirens the church bells solemnly announced the noon hour.*

Unprotected and unprepared, Manila lay under the enemy planes—a city of ancient nunneries and chromium-fronted night clubs, of skyscrapers towering over nipa [palm] shacks, of antiquity and modernity, of East and West.

. . . Something pressed between my feet. It was Cola, the office cat, her feline instincts alarmed by the sirens. Their screaming stopped, and in their place we heard the throbbing of the planes."

—Quoted in *How It Happened: World War II,* edited by Jon E. Lewis

MacArthur needed reinforcements, but U.S. military commanders back in Washington D.C. did not want to risk further losses. President Roosevelt told MacArthur to hold on for as long as possible. A siege of the Bataan peninsula followed, squeezing some 67,000 Filipino troops, over 12,000 Americans, and 26,000 civilians onto a strip of land about 25 miles (40 km) long and 20 miles (32 km) wide.

As the year 1942 began, Japan drove into the Netherlands East Indies (Indonesia), the British fell back toward Singapore, and the Americans and Filipinos dug in on the Bataan peninsula. Japanese troops, under General Masaharu Homma, attacked early in January and broke through around Mount Natib in the Philippines. The U.S. forces withdrew to a line of defense between Bagac and Orion, and forced Homma to cease further attacks. The siege that followed lasted over two months.

British General Arthur Percival (on the extreme right) on his way to sign a formal declaration of the surrender of Singapore in February 1942.

By the beginning of February, all the British-led troops were on Singapore island *(see page 8)* and another, shorter, siege began. With 70,000 soldiers, British General Arthur Percival made the mistake of trying to defend Singapore's entire northern coastline and the Japanese were able to break through. Despite having only 35,000 troops and little ammunition left, the Japanese commander, General Tomoyuki Yamashita, held on. The city of Singapore was demoralized. Some troops panicked and began to desert, and, in the middle of February, Percival surrendered to Yamashita. Churchill called it "the worst disaster and largest capitulation in British history."

Meanwhile, MacArthur had been instructed to leave Corregidor and seek safety in Australia. The troops he left behind were under orders not to surrender, but this became increasingly difficult. Food was in short supply, and malaria and other illnesses afflicted the men, which made resistance futile when the Japanese attacked once again in April. The American in charge, Major General Edward King, disobeyed MacArthur and surrendered on April 9 to save unnecessary deaths. Nearly 80,000 survivors were marched out of the peninsula on what

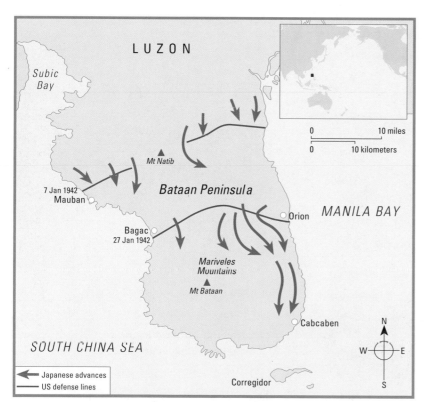

There was such a shortage of food that the defenders on Bataan were reduced to eating horses and water buffalo before surrendering to the invading Japanese forces.

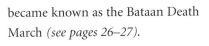

DEMORALIZED SURRENDER IN SINGAPORE

A Singaporean, Lee Kip Lin, and a British soldier, J. O. C. Hayes, were among those who witnessed the appalling lack of discipline in the final days before the surrender of Singapore: *"We drove down Orchard Road and I remember very distinctly hundreds of these soldiers . . . sprawled all over the road, drunk. And they broke into the shops opposite the Orchard Road Market . . . the streets were full of obvious deserters. They loitered in twos and threes, armed and shouting the news that 'they* [the Japanese] *won't be long now.'"*

became known as the Bataan Death March (*see pages 26–27*).

THE WAR SPREADS

By April 1942, Japan had not only conquered Malaya, Singapore, and the Philippines, but also the greater part of the Netherlands East Indies (now Indonesia). Hong Kong surrendered. The Japanesse defeated the British in southern Burma (now Myanmar) and, following the invasion of Malaya, Japan was officiallly at war with Britain. Japan and the U.S. were at war since the attack on Pearl Harbor. Since Germany had also declared war on the U.S., World War II was now a truly global conflict.

Above: The fortified island of Corregidor finally surrendered on May 7, 1942.

Left: Jubilation breaks out when Japanese soldiers are told that the U.S. and Filipino troops who were defending Bataan have surrendered.

13

CHAPTER 2

LAND AND SEA BATTLES

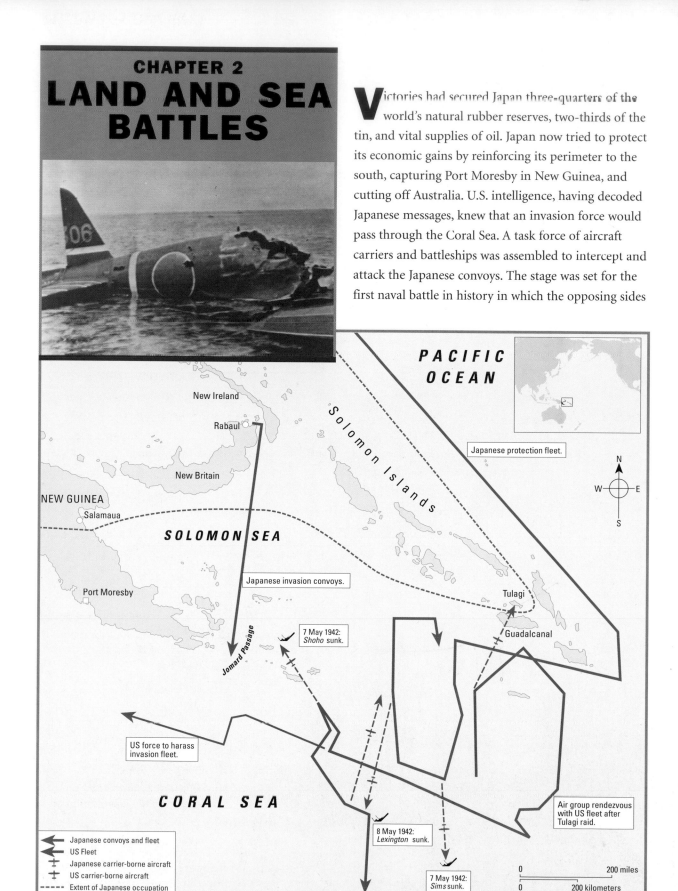

ictories had secured Japan three-quarters of the world's natural rubber reserves, two-thirds of the tin, and vital supplies of oil. Japan now tried to protect its economic gains by reinforcing its perimeter to the south, capturing Port Moresby in New Guinea, and cutting off Australia. U.S. intelligence, having decoded Japanese messages, knew that an invasion force would pass through the Coral Sea. A task force of aircraft carriers and battleships was assembled to intercept and attack the Japanese convoys. The stage was set for the first naval battle in history in which the opposing sides

PACIFIC OCEAN

New Ireland

Rabaul

New Britain

NEW GUINEA

Salamaua

SOLOMON SEA

Solomon Islands

Japanese protection fleet.

Port Moresby

Japanese invasion convoys.

Tulagi

Guadalcanal

Jomard Passage

7 May 1942: *Shoho* sunk.

US force to harass invasion fleet.

Air group rendezvous with US fleet after Tulagi raid.

CORAL SEA

8 May 1942: *Lexington* sunk.

7 May 1942: *Sims* sunk.

Japanese convoys and fleet
US Fleet
Japanese carrier-borne aircraft
US carrier-borne aircraft
Extent of Japanese occupation

0 — 200 miles
0 — 200 kilometers

The battle of the Coral Sea was fought May 4 – 8, 1942 between U.S. and Japanese navies.

never sighted one another, but relied on scout aircraft to direct attacks against one another's warships from the air.

The Japanese carriers *Shokaku* and the *Zuikaku* were sister ships that, along with destroyers and cruisers, protected the invasion convoys planning to land men at Port Moresby and Tulagi in the Solomon Islands. The convoys also had their own light carrier, the *Shoho*. On May 5, 1942, the U.S. force assembled about 404 miles (650 km) south of Guadalcanal. Two days earlier, Japanese ships landing at Tulagi had been attacked, but the U.S. plan now was to head for the Jomard Passage and to intercept the main Japanese invasion convoy.

BATTLE AT SEA

On May 7, 1942, U.S. scout aircraft spotted the convoy, which then turned back to wait and see what would happen. The *Shoho* was attacked and sunk by aircraft from the USS *Lexington*

and *Yorktown*. Japanese scout planes, like U.S. scouts earlier that day, could not find the enemy aircraft carriers, but they did find and sink the destroyer USS *Sims*.

On May 8, both sides located one another and launched full air strikes from their carriers. While equal in numbers, the Japanese had the superior Mitsubishi A6M Zero fighter and sank the *Lexington* by striking it with bombs and torpedoes. The *Yorktown* was damaged. The *Shokaku* was also damaged but the *Zuikaku* was never located.

In one sense, the result of the haphazard battle of the Coral Sea was a tie—both sides suffered losses but neither side was dealt a knockout blow. In the long run, however, the U.S. forces could be pleased with the result: The enemy's attempt to capture Port Morseby was blocked and, with one carrier sunk and another badly damaged, the Japanese were weakened in advance of the next and more decisive sea battle that was about to take place.

BATTLE OF THE CORAL SEA

U.S. aircraft carriers	2	Lost	1
Japanese aircraft carriers	3	Lost	1
U.S. cruisers	5	Lost	0
Japanese cruisers	6	Lost	0
U.S. destroyers	9	Lost	1
Japanese destroyers	7	Lost	0

—From *The Second World War in the East*, H.P. Willmott

Opposite page: A Japanese fighter is shot down during the battle of the Coral Sea; and (below) the *Shokaku* is on fire and taking evasive action during the same battle.

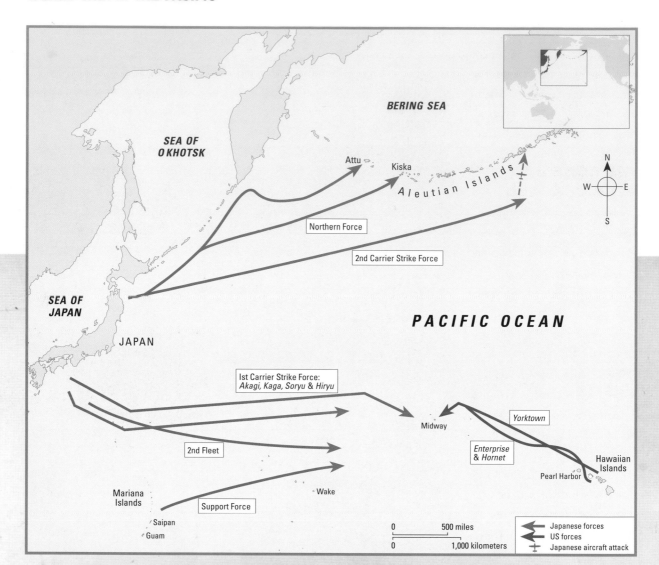

BERING SEA

SEA OF OKHOTSK

Attu
Kiska
Aleutian Islands

Northern Force

2nd Carrier Strike Force

SEA OF JAPAN

JAPAN

PACIFIC OCEAN

1st Carrier Strike Force: *Akagi, Kaga, Soryu & Hiryu*

Yorktown

Midway

Enterprise & Hornet

2nd Fleet

Hawaiian Islands

Pearl Harbor

Mariana Islands

Wake

Saipan

Guam

Support Force

| 0 | | 500 miles |
| 0 | | 1,000 kilometers |

Japanese forces
US forces
Japanese aircraft attack

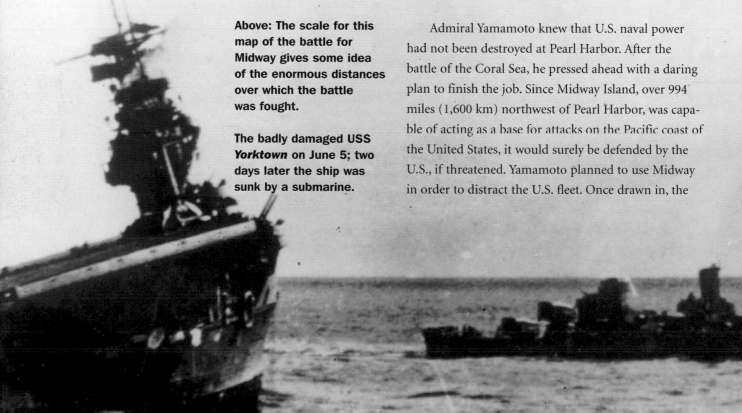

Above: The scale for this map of the battle for Midway gives some idea of the enormous distances over which the battle was fought.

The badly damaged USS *Yorktown* on June 5; two days later the ship was sunk by a submarine.

Admiral Yamamoto knew that U.S. naval power had not been destroyed at Pearl Harbor. After the battle of the Coral Sea, he pressed ahead with a daring plan to finish the job. Since Midway Island, over 994 miles (1,600 km) northwest of Pearl Harbor, was capable of acting as a base for attacks on the Pacific coast of the United States, it would surely be defended by the U.S., if threatened. Yamamoto planned to use Midway in order to distract the U.S. fleet. Once drawn in, the larger number of Japanese aircraft carriers, battleships, and destroyers lying in wait could destroy the enemy fleet. The plan also called for a smaller attack on the Aleutian Islands, north of Midway, as a diversion to split the U.S. fleet.

THE CODE HAD BEEN CRACKED

What Yamamoto did not know was that coded Japanese radio messages had been cracked, and Admiral Chester W. Nimitz, commander of the U.S. Pacific Fleet, was aware of the plan. Early on June 4, 1942, Japanese carrier aircraft attacked Midway. Their carrier fleet was located by U.S. aircraft from the *Yorktown*, but their early attacks failed and thirty-five U.S. planes were lost. Then U.S. Admiral Raymond A. Spruance, with the *Enterprise* and *Hornet*, took the opportunity for a surprise attack. Three Japanese carriers were caught while they were refuelling after attacking Midway. A small group of U.S. dive-bombers targeted the carriers. Their defenders were in disarray, and they were quickly turned into burning wrecks.

A fourth Japanese carrier, *Hiryu*, escaped and was able to join in an attack on the *Yorktown* on the afternoon of the same day. The seriously damaged *Yorktown* would later be sunk by a Japanese submarine, but *Hiryu* was also damaged beyond repair. Spruance then chose to withdraw, which was just as well because there was another Japanese force advancing on Midway under Admiral Yamamoto.

In the end, the battle of Midway was the first decisive defeat of the Japanese in the Pacific. It signaled a shift in the balance of power in favor of the U.S., although this was not recognized at the time. The Japanese lost four carriers, 225 aircraft, and a cruiser;

A Farewell Drink

Japanese Admiral Kusaka recalled the last moments on board *Hiryu*: *"When it was ascertained that the ship was in a sinking condition, Admiral Yamaguchi and Captain Kaku decided that they would go down with the ship. They all shared some naval biscuits and drank a glass of water in a last ceremony. Admiral Yamaguchi gave his hat to one of his staff officers and asked him to give it to his family; then there was some joking among them— the captain and the admiral—that their duties were finished when the ship sank."*
–From *The Pacific Campaign*, Dan Van der Vat

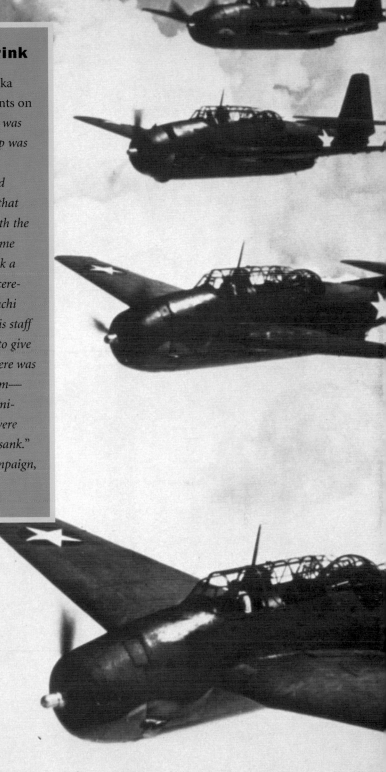

Carrier-based torpedo bombers, such as these U.S. Navy Avengers, played an important part in the naval battles of the Pacific War.

the U.S. lost one carrier, 146 planes, and a destroyer. Hundreds of lives were lost on both sides.

The Solomon Islands *(see page 14)* stretch for about 621 miles (1,000 km) across the South Pacific. The Japanese had a base there at Rabaul and a smaller presence on Tulagi and Guadalcanal. After the battle of Midway, neither side had gained control of the South Pacific and so the island of Guadalcanal became a battleground for the continuing struggle between Japan and the U.S.

The battle started on August 7, 1942, when 10,000 U.S. troops landed on Guadalcanal. Then Japanese warships from Rabaul appeared unexpectedly off neighboring Savo Island and sank four cruisers sent there to protect the landings. More than 1,000 Allied seamen lost their lives in the Slot, a seaway area between the Florida Islands and Guadalcanal that

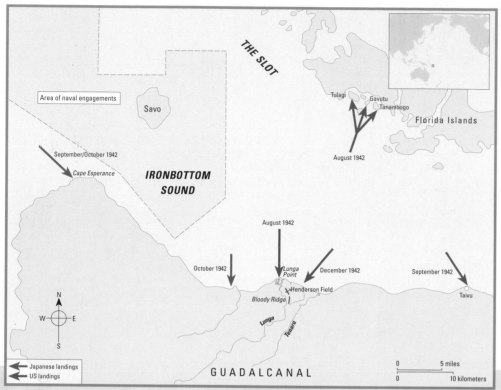

Map labels:
THE SLOT

Area of naval engagements

Savo

September/October 1942

Cape Esperance

IRONBOTTOM SOUND

Tulagi
Gavutu
Tanambogo
Florida Islands

August 1942

August 1942

October 1942

Lunga Point

December 1942

September 1942

Henderson Field
Bloody Ridge
Taivu

Lunga
Tenaru

N
W—E
S

GUADALCANAL

→ Japanese landings
→ US landings

0   5 miles
0   10 kilometers

Left: The land battle for Guadalcanal was mostly restricted to a relatively small area around Henderson Field.

Below: U.S. Marines rush ashore from a landing craft to join the battle on Guadalcanal.

U.S. Marines examine a Japanese machine-gun emplacement in the malaria-ridden jungle on the island of Guadalcanal.

became known as Ironbottom Sound because of all the ships that were sunk there. The Japanese then chose to withdraw rather than stay and attack the transport ships, to avoid the risk of counterattacks from the air.

THE BATTLE FOR GUADALCANAL

The island of New Guinea *(see page 20)* and its capital Port Moresby, north of Australia, also became part of the struggle for control of the southwest Pacific. Troops on Guadalcanal were left unprotected and undersupplied, but they did complete an unfinished Japanese airfield on the north coast. Named Henderson Field, it became a target for the Japanese when they landed their own troops on the island. Between September and November, each side was reinforced with thousands more soldiers who fought desperately in a series of engagements, with Japanese troops advancing to within about 985 yards (900 m) of the airfield in the battle of Bloody Ridge in September.

The land battles were accompanied by a series of seven naval engagements. In November, a three-day sea battle unfolded as the Japanese attempted to land fresh troops while aircraft from Henderson Field attacked them. No single engagement proved conclusive over five months of fighting, but the U.S. forces gradually took control. By January 1943, they had about 50,000 troops on the island. Finally, the remaining Japanese, more than 10,000 of them, were evacuated from the island at night without being spotted by their enemy.

With the battle for Guadalcanal, close-combat fighting in tropical jungle conditions become a feature of the Pacific War. The island, in its own right, was not worth the losses that both sides suffered, but in the

long run this was the first successful U.S. land battle in the Pacific, and it marked a turning point in the war. Australians became heavily involved in the fighting, in

LOSSES AT GUADALCANAL

Naval engagements, 12–14 November 1942

U.S. battleships	2	Lost 0
Japanese battleships	3	Lost 2
U.S. heavy cruisers	2	Lost 0
Japanese heavy cruisers	2	Lost 0
U.S. light cruisers	2	Lost 0
Japanese light cruisers	3	Lost 0
U.S. destroyers	12	Lost 6
Japanese destroyers	19	Lost 3

Land engagements, August 1942–February 1943

U.S. troops	60,000
Killed	1,600
Japanese troops	36,000
Killed/missing	15,000
Died of sickness	10,000

—From *The Second World War in the East,* H.P. Willmott

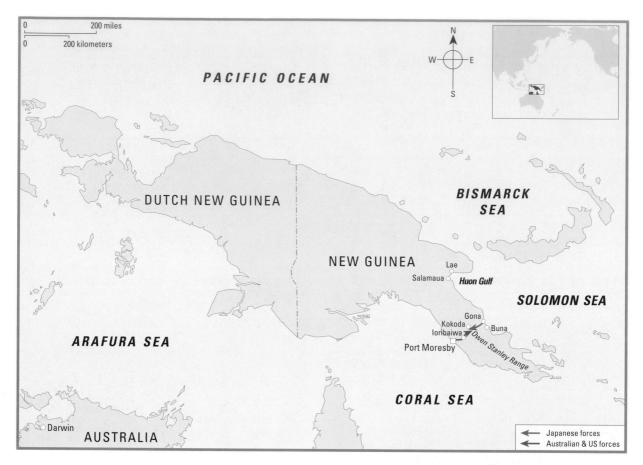

Above: New Guinea was divided into a Dutch half (part of the Netherlands East Indies) and an Australian-controlled half.

part because their own country was coming under Japanese threat. By October 1943, nearly half a million Australian infantry were in the Pacific, under U.S. control, compared with fewer than 200,000 U.S. land troops.

Japanese forces had landed on the northern coast of New Guinea in March 1942. They intended to move overland and capture Port Moresby, but the Battle of the Coral Sea interrupted this operation. After the Battle of Midway, the U.S. felt confident enough to try to clear this Japanese force. General MacArthur was in command as Australian troops moved north from Port Moresby to engage the enemy. Meanwhile, on July 12, 1942, more Japanese landed on the northern coast and moved south. There was only one route across the 13,124 foot (4,000 m) high Owen Stanley mountains that divided Port Moresby from the north coast. It was an almost impassable mud track through jungle and over high ridges known as the Kokoda Trail. It became

General MacArthur passes Australian troops on their way to fight in northern New Guinea.

a desperate battleground as Japanese and Australian soldiers fought one another and struggled to survive in the jungle. Soldiers who lost the trail died and many Japanese also starved to death because of inadequate supplies of food.

Fighting over the Kokoda Trail lasted until the Japanese withdrew in September. Australians and U.S. troops then attacked Gona and Buna, but it was not until January 1943 that the area was cleared of

MARCHING IN THE JUNGLE

Ogawa Masatsugu, a Japanese soldier, remembers the campaign in New Guinea and the terrible conditions that drove many soldiers to suicide: *"It rained for more than half a year straight. Our guns rusted. Iron just rotted way. Wounds wouldn't heal . . . You slipped and fell, got up, went sprawling, stood up, like an army of marching mud dolls. It went on without end, just trudging through the muddy water, following the legs of someone in front of you . . . All battlefields are wretched places. New Guinea was ghastly. There was a saying during the war: 'Burma is hell; from New Guinea no one returns alive.'*
. . . In the army, anyone over thirty was an old man. Twenty-six or twenty-seven, that was your peak. The young soldiers, serving for the first time, didn't know how to pace themselves and died quickly, though there were many strong men, fishermen and farmers, among them."
—From *Japan At War*, Haruko Taya Cook and Theodore F. Cook

The bodies of slain American soldiers lie on the beach at Buna on the northeast coast of New Guinea, January 1943.

Japanese troops. Meanwhile, from Lae and Salamaua on the northwest coast, another Japanese advance on Port Moresby got under way. By the end of February, it had been driven back. Japanese forces had been stretched in New Guinea because the battle for Guadalcanal was taking place at the same time.

CHAPTER 3
THE VICTIMS

Chinese civilians flee for their lives during a Japanese bombing raid on Canton in 1938.

Japan's rapid victories in the first half of 1942 established a new empire that stretched for thousands of miles (kilometers), from mainland China to far-flung Pacific islands. It affected the lives of millions of ordinary citizens. Japan proclaimed the creation of a *Greater East Asia Coprosperity Scheme* that would liberate Asians from white colonial rule. At first, many people in the occupied countries welcomed this idea and saw the Japanese as liberators. In Sumatra, local people rose in rebellion against their Dutch rulers

Below: Japan, having conquered a vast area, faced the problem of keeping it under Japanese control during the Pacific War.

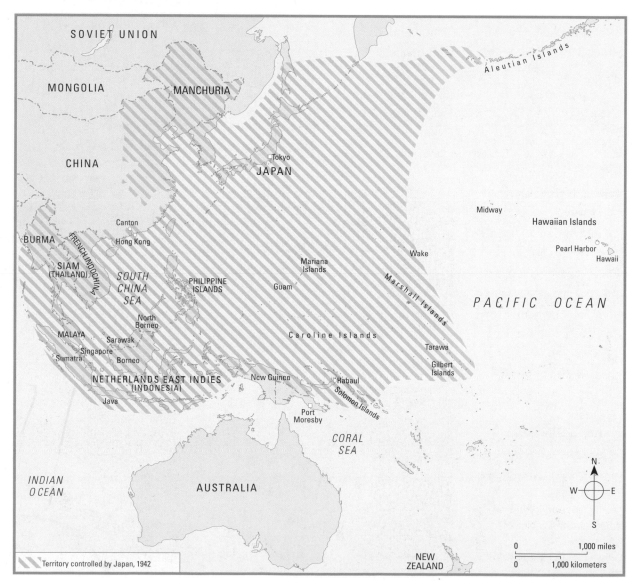

Territory controlled by Japan, 1942

and arrested those who tried to flee before the Japanese arrived. Later, peasants were forced into slave labor by the Japanese, and an estimated four million people died as a result of the Japanese occupation of the Netherlands East Indies (now Indonesia).

While the Japanese were fighting in China, they suspected Chinese who were living overseas of supporting their enemy. In Singapore, many thousands of Chinese were driven to beaches and machine-gunned by Japanese soldiers. It was not only the Chinese who were harshly treated. An estimated 200,000 women, mostly Korean but also Filipinos and some Dutch, were drafted into camps where they became "comfort women," forced to provide sex for Japanese soldiers.

Neither the Japanese nor the Allies respected the culture of Pacific Islanders and the Islanders suffered terribly as a result. Many were forced to work and fight for the opposing armies, meaning they could end up killing one another. Their traditional way of life came under severe stress as they struggled to cope: "All the clans . . . who were once brave, courageous, and strong seemed to become like babies in their first day out of their mother's wombs. The landings of the Japanese, gun noises, and the actual sight of the ships . . . They could not run . . . It was a unique disaster beyond anybody's memory," recorded a New Guinean man. New Guineans died in tens of thousands as their land was bombed.

Japanese victories between December 1941 and April 1942 led to huge num-

Pacific Islanders, like these on Guadalcanal helping U.S. troops build an airfield runway, became involved in the conflict in various ways.

NOWHERE TO RUN

Pacific Islanders had no choice but to endure the battles that erupted on their islands. One man describes how they tried to survive: *"All of us were in holes … We were hungry and thirsty, but no one could go out. If you traveled outside you would disappear . . . Then in their coming the [American] warriors were not straight in their working. They came to the shelter of ours, guns ready, and looked toward us inside. So great was our fear that we were all in a corner, like kittens. And then they yelled and threw in a hand grenade . . . When it burst, the whole shelter was torn apart . . . Earth fragments struck us, but the others in the other half, they died."*
—From *The Second World War: A People's History*, Joanna Bourke

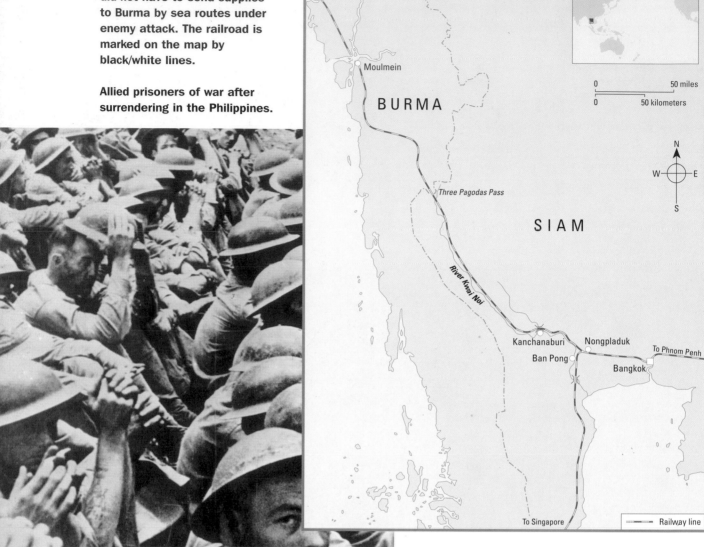

Right: The Japanese built the Burma-Siam Railway so that they did not have to send supplies to Burma by sea routes under enemy attack. The railroad is marked on the map by black/white lines.

Allied prisoners of war after surrendering in the Philippines.

bers of soldiers and European civilians being taken prisoner. About 70,000 troops surrendered in Singapore, as well as 10,000 U.S. soldiers and 62,000 Filipinos on the Bataan peninsula. Most of the quarter of a million Dutch nationals in the Netherlands East Indies (now Indonesia), the 3,000 British in Hong Kong, and the 4,500 British in Singapore, including about three hundred children, were interned. Many did not survive the harsh conditions, poor diet, and lack of medical facilities in the prison camps.

FORCED INTO SLAVE LABOR

Forced to work on railroads, coal mines, roads, docks, and factories, prisoners' food rations kept them barely alive. Millions of peasants were forced into slave labor on Java, and in Siam (now Thailand) the Japanese used prisoners of war (POWs) and civilians to dig a railway line to Burma (now Myanmar) through 260 miles (420 km) of mountainous jungle. About 300,000 Asians from Malaya (now Malaysia), Burma, and the Netherlands East Indies were brought to work on the railway line, having no idea of the starvation diet and brutal conditions awaiting them. In addition, 60,000 Australian, British, and Dutch POWs were transported to Siam to work on the railway.

"I DO NOT WANT TO KNOW HOW MY FATHER DIED"

Greta Kwik from Holland was a 16-year-old girl living in Java when the Japanese invaded the island. She recorded her memories fifty years later: *"I may still have the piece of paper on which Queen Wilhelmina of the Netherlands wrote that she was sorry about what happened. I never looked for it because everything still hurts. When we received it, much, much later, it finally dawned on me that my father was dead. I remember crying and banging my head against a wall in utter sorrow. I do not want to know how my father died. Was he standing, blindfolded, and shot? Did he have to kneel, hands bound behind his back, and have his head chopped off, to topple in a grave of his own digging? . . . I have waited for my father all my life . . . For most of the past 50 years, I have shed a tear every January 29, his execution date."*

—From *The Second World War: A People's History*, Joanna Bourke

Many POWs in Japanese camps, kept alive with the barest minimum of food but still expected to work hard, never survived their ordeal.

Conditions were awful for everyone, but Asians, including many women and children, suffered the worst. As many as one in three died, compared to one in five Allied prisoners of war. Dr. Hardie, a POW working on the Burma-Siam Railway, kept a secret diary about Asian prisoners: "People who have been near these camps speak with bated breath of the state of affairs—corpses rotting unburied in the jungle, almost complete lack of sanitation, a frightful stench, overcrowding, swarms of flies."

The Pacific War was an especially vicious conflict and part of the reason for this lies in a deep-rooted racism and nationalism that marked the attitudes of the countries fighting one another.

BATAAN DEATH MARCH

William Dyess survived the death march but realized how people become used to brutality:

"Their ferocity grew as we marched on into the afternoon . . . I stumbled over a man writhing in the hot dust of the road. He was a Filipino soldier who had been bayoneted through his stomach. Within a quarter of a mile I walked past another. This soldier prisoner had been rolled into the path of the trucks and crushed beneath the heavy wheels. The huddled and smashed figures beside the road eventually became commonplace to us. The human mind has an amazing faculty of adjusting to shock."

–From *How It Happened: World War II*, Jon E. Lewis. editor

Many Japanese believed (with some historical reasons) that Europe and the U.S. wanted to make colonies out of all of Asia. Westerners were seen as enemies in racial terms, hypocrites who would not admit to their own greed in wanting to control Asia. Racist and nationalistic attitudes took hold as Japan's own ambitions in Asia were blocked by the U.S. The views of military leaders who accused the United States and Britain of imperialism gained influence in Japan. Many Japanese also felt that those in the U.S. and Britain wanted to humiliate the Japanese people by not accepting them as equals.

Allied prisoners of war during the Bataan Death March; of those who survived the march, another 16,000 died in the first few weeks at their destination camp.

ATTITUDES AND THE BRUTALITY OF WAR
The Japanese military code of conduct did not accept honorable surrender. Japanese soldiers were encouraged to see themselves as noble warriors fighting a corrupt enemy, and an enemy who surrendered was next to worthless. Evidence of this brutal attitude came after the surrender of U.S. and Philippine forces on the Bataan peninsula in 1942. Forced to march around sixty-five miles (105 km) to a prison camp, the prisoners were clubbed and bayoneted along the way. Five to ten thousand Filipinos and over six hundred Americans died on the trek, many from exhaustion and starvation.

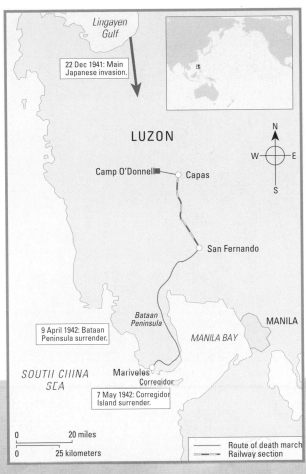

Lingayen
Gulf

22 Dec 1941: Main
Japanese invasion.

LUZON

Camp O'Donnell▪ ━━○ Capas

○ San Fernando

Bataan
Peninsula

MANILA

9 April 1942: Bataan
Peninsula surrender.

MANILA BAY

*SOUTH CHINA
SEA*

Mariveles
Corregidor

7 May 1942: Corregidor
Island surrender.

0 ━━━━ 20 miles
0 ━━━━ 25 kilometers

━━━ Route of death march
═══ Railway section

Above: The Bataan Death March forced prisoners of war up the Bataan peninsula and well inland to the former Philippine Army Camp O'Donnell, about 65 miles (105 km) to the north.

A belief in their own racial superiority was shared by many U.S., European, and Australian forces. Air Chief Marshal Sir Robert Brooke-Popham, commander of British forces in southeast Asia, described how in 1940: "I had a good closeup, across the barbed wire, of various subhuman specimens dressed in dirty grey uniform, which I was informed were Japanese soldiers." Similarly, a U.S. general congratulated his troops: "The sincere admiration of the entire Third Fleet is yours for the hill-blasting, cave-smashing extermination of 11,000 slant-eyed gophers." Many Pacific War soldiers had no previous experience of battle. They were young men who had volunteered or were conscripted for service, and the reality of combat was a terrible experience. The death of friends and

Below: A Japanese soldier, bayonet at the ready, guards Allied prisoners during their forced march up the Bataan peninsula.

fellow soldiers was awful and it hardened attitudes towards the enemy. One U.S. soldier, George Peto, remembered how, after the death of a friend, " . . . that sure put a different perspective on my part in the war." Peto went on to say that it changed and hardened his attitude towards the enemy and, in a similar kind of way, after the surrender on the Bataan peninsula, one group of prisoners were told by a Japanese officer that " . . . we're going to kill you because you killed many of our soldiers." For soldiers on both sides, the war became personal and vengeful.

Atrocities against soldiers and civilians were committed by both

"A KILLING MACHINE"

Nelson Perry, an American soldier, remembers how the Pacific war turned ordinary individuals into something else when in battle: *"Men in combat … cease being individuals; they become part of a machine that kills and that bayonets people, that sets fire to people, that laughs at people when they're running down the trail screaming in agony and you laugh at them. It's because you're no longer an individual, you're part of a machine, a killing machine."*

Yamauchi Taeko, who surrendered on Saipan, made a similar observation: *"The American soldiers had been demons on the battlefield, ready to kill me in an instant. Now here they were, right in front of my eyes. Relaxed. Sprawled on top of jeeps, shouting, 'Hey!' Joking with each other."*

—From *Hell in the Pacific*, Jonathan Lewis and Ben Steele, and *Japan At War*, Haruko Taya Cook and Theodore F. Cook

An American medic on Saipan; wounded soldiers were evacuated to hospital ships waiting offshore.

U.S. soldiers remember and mourn their fallen comrades on Saipan.

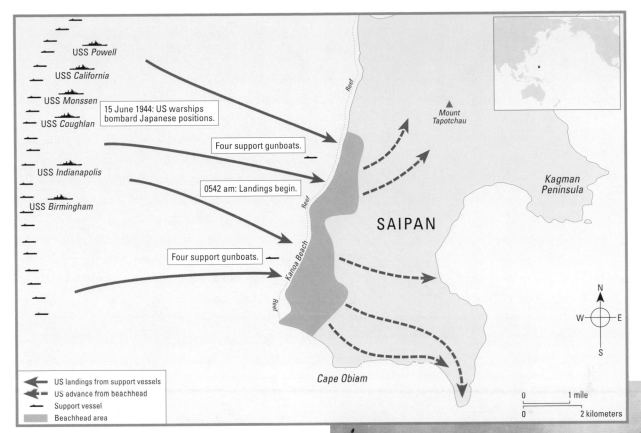

US landings from support vessels
US advance from beachhead
Support vessel
Beachhead area

USS *Powell*
USS *California*
USS *Monssen*
USS *Coughlan*
USS *Indianapolis*
USS *Birmingham*

15 June 1944: US warships bombard Japanese positions.

Four support gunboats.

0542 am: Landings begin.

Four support gunboats.

Reef

Mount Tapotchau

SAIPAN

Kagman Peninsula

Kanoa Beach

Cape Obiam

0   1 mile
0   2 kilometers

N
W   E
S

Above: Japanese resistance on Saipan was fierce, despite intense bombardment by U.S. battleships for two days before the landings.

Right: Determined Japanese forces dug out defensive positions on Saipan that U.S. troops had to destroy one by one.

sides. It was not unusual for captured soldiers to be killed rather than taken prisoner. The capture of the Japanese-controlled island of Saipan in the Marianas involved ferocious fighting that illustrates just how vicious the Pacific war became. U.S. troops landed on the island—which was 14 miles long (22 km)—in mid-June 1944. They had planned three days for the island's capture, but fierce Japanese resistance stretched this into three weeks. Some four thousand Americans were killed or injured on the beaches in the first two days. The Japanese then withdrew to a rocky area around Mount Tapotchau.

One night early in July, Japanese infantry troops launched a desperate all-out attack, known as a *banzai*. Advancing regardless of the enemy's answering fire, the *banzai* soon turned into a suicidal attack. As many as

four thousand Japanese may have lost their lives in this one action. A few days later, thousands of Japanese civilians living on the island jumped off the cliffs in defiance of a U.S. victory. Nearly 8,000 civilians died on Saipan, bringing total Japanese losses to more than 30,000; U.S. dead totaled 3,426.

CHAPTER 4
FIGHTING BACK

Above: The raising of the U.S. flag on one of the Solomon Islands symbolized the successful expulsion of Japanese forces by U.S. troops.

Early in 1943, with Guadalcanal captured and the enemy being forced off New Guinea, the U.S. troops felt confident enough to push forward with their plan to capture the main Japanese base at Rabaul on New Britain. Troops landed on New Georgia at the end of June, but it was August 5 before the island's airfield was captured. There were battles at sea as well as fierce fighting on land that took their toll of these U.S. troops who were not yet battle-hardened.

By the middle of August, flights from New Georgia's airfield supported new landings on the neighboring island of Vella Lavella. More than one thousand Americans lost their lives taking the two islands and more than twice that number of Japanese died on New Georgia alone. By November, U.S. troops had landed on Bougainville and the following month saw landings on the Green Islands. Rabaul, however, was heavily defended by Japanese soldiers living in specially built tunnels. A land attack was delayed and the island of New Britain was bombed heavily from the air until the Japanese garrison was put out of action.

Both the U.S. Army under General MacArthur and the U.S. Navy under Admiral Nimitz were in action against the Japanese. There was a certain amount of rivalry between the two forces, but it never became a

Below: An assault boat carries U.S. Marines to land at Empress Augusta Bay on November 1, 1943, at the start of a hard-fought campaign to clear Bougainville Island of its Japanese garrison.

Map

PACIFIC OCEAN

Rabaul

Green Islands

New Britain

Bougainville

Choiseul

SOLOMON SEA

Vella Lavella

New Georgia

Russell Island

NEW GUINEA

Henderson Field

Guadalcanal

CORAL SEA

Solomon Islands

N
W — E
S

0   200 miles
0   250 kilometers

← US offensive

This map shows the main theaters of war as U.S. and Japanese forces wrestled for control of the Solomons.

PA 27

U.S. troops survey bodies of enemy soldiers killed on a Guadalcanal beach after an unsuccessful Japanese attempt to land reinforcements.

serious problem. Both commanders were helped by the fact that, by the end of 1943, the U.S. war economy rolled new aircraft, tanks, and ships off the production lines in record time. By early 1944, a new aircraft was completed every 294 seconds. Also, U.S. submarines, sailing from Pearl Harbor and Australian bases, achieved increasing success against enemy shipping. The Japanese

TORMENTS OF WAR

Ogawa Tamotsu, a Japanese medic, was ordered to kill patients who were too ill to care for:

"I was at the front almost six years, in China, and then in the South Pacific. The final year was the most horrible. It was just a hell. I was a medic in a field hospital on New Britain Island . . . We were five or six medics with one to two hundred patients to care for . . . In the beginning it was hard to do it, then I got used to it and didn't cry any more. I became a murderer . . . Sometimes, when I look back, I even get a sense of fulfilment that I survived. Sometimes, though, it's all nothingness. I think to myself: 'I deserve a death sentence. I didn't kill just one or two.' Only war allows this—these torments I have to bear until I die. My war will continue until that moment."

—From *Japan at War*, Haruko Taya Cook and Theodore F. Cook

A U.S. Marine hurls a grenade at a Japanese machine-gun post during the grim battle for Tarawa in November 1943.

found it difficult to maintain supply lines, seriously weakening their ability to keep fighting the war.

A KILLING ZONE
The south-to-north advance on Japan, through New Guinea and eventually the Philippines, was under the command of General MacArthur. Admiral Nimitz preferred an "island hopping" strategy, starting in the Central Pacific and continuing through the Caroline Islands and the Marianas, before pushing close to Japan through Iwo Jima and Okinawa. After the decision to bypass Rabaul in the southwest, the drive toward Japan shifted to the Central Pacific. Nimitz's campaign began with the Tarawa Atoll in the Gilbert Islands.

Triangular in shape and nowhere rising much more than 11 feet (3.5 m) above sea level, Tarawa is one of 16 atolls forming the Gilbert Islands. It is made up of 47 coral islands, the largest of which, Betio, is only about 2.5 miles (4 km) long. Tarawa Atoll was invaded in November 1943. The landing area, divided into zones called Red 1, 2 and 3 by the U.S., was expertly protected by nearly 5,000 elite troops under Japanese Rear Admiral Shibasaki. A coconut log barricade about 10 feet (3 m) high, held together with steel clamps, was constructed off the shore line to channel the invaders into a killing zone. Here, U.S. troops faced heavy gunfire from emplacements dug in behind timber, sand, and also concrete defenses. The Allies fired tons of shells at the island's defenders but they had little effect. The Japanese were able to fire at will at the

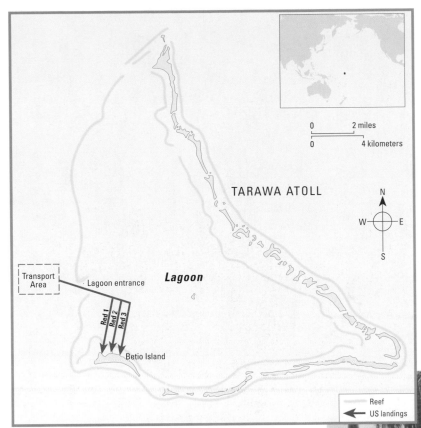

TARAWA ATOLL

Lagoon

Transport Area

Lagoon entrance

Red 1 Red 2 Red 3

Betio Island

0   2 miles
0   4 kilometers

N
W   E
S

Reef
US landings

the end of the third day the island was taken. U.S. Army casualty figures reported that only 17 Japanese prisoners, out of a garrison force of 4,836, survived the fierce battle for Tarawa. U.S. dead numbered more than eight hundred, with more than two thousand injured.

Left: U.S. troops and Japanese fought bitterly for possession of the coral island of Betio, part of Tarawa atoll. It is no larger than New York City's Central Park.

Below: U.S. forces advancing in Tarawa, one of the most heavily fortified islands fought over during the Pacific War.

troops who were forced to wade ashore, since Allied landing craft could not pass the natural defense of the coral reef.

It was not until the second day, when U.S. troops occupied part of the south shore and an area in the west, that reinforcements were able to land there. The Japanese eventually withdrew to the eastern end of the island and counterattacked with *banzai* charges, but by

"OUR ONLY ARMOUR WAS THE SHIRT ON OUR BACKS"

Bob Libby should have landed on Red 1, but his launch hit the coral reef and he leaped overboard:
"The sound of screaming shells passed overhead, the unmistakeable crack of rifle fire zipped around our ears, heavy explosions on shore . . . the screams of the wounded were lost in this cacophony of sound—all the while we who survived so far still made our way to the beach to find some haven of safety, if such existed . . . Every step of the way was a life and death situation; how anyone ever reached the shore is still mysterious to me as the enemy fire seemed to cover every inch between the reef and shore – there was no hiding place, no protection, our only armour was the shirt on our backs."

—From *Tarawa–A Hell of a Way to Die*, Derrick Wright

WORLD WAR II: THE PACIFIC

After Tarawa, the next objective was the Marshall Islands, a group of thirty-six Central Pacific atolls. U.S. intelligence had decoded messages that indicated that the Japanese expected an attack on the Marshall's outer atolls. Instead, these atolls were weakened by bombing attacks from Tarawa and bypassed, not surrendering until the end of the war. U.S. troops landed on Majura atoll on January 30, 1944—the first U.S. occupation of pre-war Japanese land—and in mid-February they successfully attacked the more heavily defended Eniwetok both from the air and by land. In February, the U.S. Navy attacked the Japanese naval base of Truk, one of the Caroline Islands, dropping thirty times more explosives on that target than the Japanese had dropped on Pearl Harbor.

General MacArthur, not to be outdone by Admiral

After the capture of the Marshall and Caroline Islands, the Mariana Islands were the next target.

Above: A large transport vessel lands U.S. troops in the Marshall Islands in April 1944.

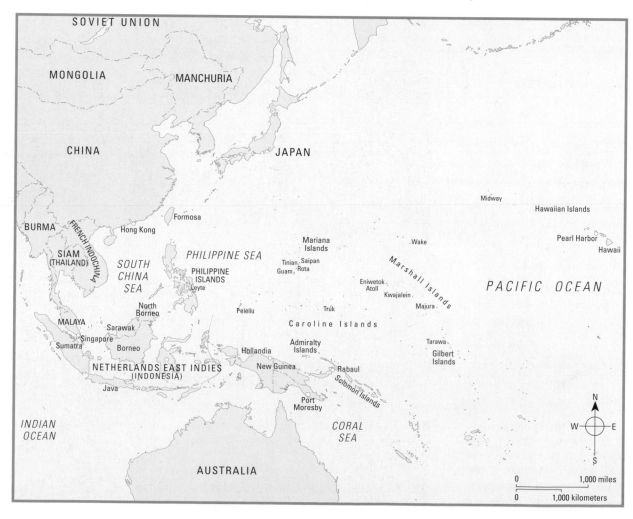

Nimitz, captured the Admiralty Islands in the soutwest and then seized Hollandia. Decoding enemy messages allowed his forces to leap over pockets of Japanese resistance, leaving them ineffective.

THE CENTRAL PACIFIC

In the Central Pacific, the way was open for an attack on the Mariana Islands: Saipan, Tinian, Rota, and Guam being the main targets. U.S forces launched invasions in February 1944, and in August Guam was the last of the islands to be taken. The Japanese mounted a strike force of nine aircraft carriers to repel the invaders in what became the battle of the Philippine Sea in June. It was the biggest carrier battle of the war. The Japanese were the first to locate their enemy but their pilots were outnumbered and outmatched by U.S. fighters. The next day, the Japanese fleet was located; one carrier was sunk and three damaged. U.S. submarines had already sunk two others.

After the capture of the Mariana Islands, U.S. commanders had to decide whether to move closer to Japan via Formosa or take back the Philippines. MacArthur and Nimitz agreed on the Philippines and planned to seize the Japanese-occupied coral island of Peleliu as protection for landings on Leyte in the Philippines. The capture of Peleliu turned into one of the war's bloodiest engagements, starting on September 15 and not ending until the end of November.

The Japanese knew that it was important to try to prevent the capture of the Philippines

U.S. soldiers celebrate the capture of the Eniwetok atoll in the Marshall Islands, which brought U.S. aircraft within range of the Caroline Islands.

THE FORGOTTEN BATTLE

Equal in ferocity to the battle for Tarawa, the struggle for Peleliu received far less publicity during the war. Regarded as the Pacific War's "forgotten battle," it is debatable whether it should ever have been fought. It made little difference to the capture of the Philippines and the human cost was terrible:

U.S.
1,050 killed in action
150 died of wounds
5,450 wounded
36 missing

Japanese
10,900 killed
202 prisoners; 19 of whom were Japanese, the rest being non-Japanese laborers

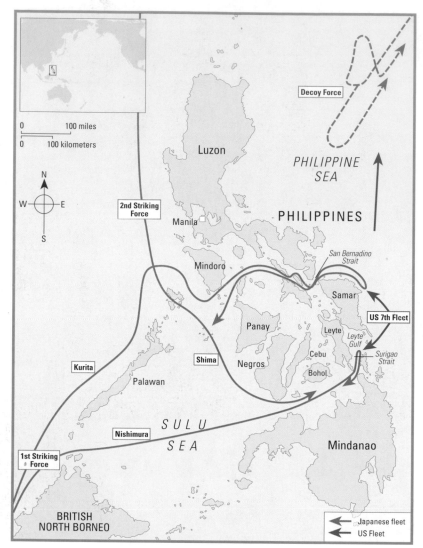

Above: The Japanese First Striking Force split, with Nishimura heading east towards Leyte and Kurita heading northeast.

Above: Admiral Jizaburo Ozawa (1886–1963) played a successful part in the Leyte Gulf battle.

two of them and wiped out along with their support ships.

THE BATTLE OF LEYTE GULF

The Japanese plan failed, partly because Nishimura's force was virtually destroyed by U.S. battleships and cruisers, and Shima, who was following behind, withdrew without joining the fight. The other, stronger force, under Kurita, was met the following morning, and the battle that followed was hardfought on both sides. For the first time, *kamikaze* pilots, suicidally crashing their aircraft onto their targets, sank an U.S. ship. The outcome of the battle seemed to be in doubt when, to the surprise and relief of the Americans, Kurita withdrew.

Choosing to engage the enemy in the battle of Leyte Gulf, the largest naval battle in world history, was a necessary gamble for the Japanese. Without the Philippines, they would be cut off from their fuel supplies in the Netherlands East Indies (now Indonesia). The gamble failed. The Japanese lost most of the major naval ships that they possessed and ten

and so halt the U.S. advance towards their home country. The plan was that Vice Admiral Jizaburo Ozawa, in overall command of the operation, would divert the main U.S. force by sailing four almost empty aircraft carriers to the northeast of the Philippines. The bulk of the Japanese naval force—comprising most of the Japanese warships still afloat—would be split between Vice Admirals Kiyohide Shima and Takeo Kurita. Shima, aided by some of Kurita's ships under the command of Vice Admiral Shoji Nishimura, would occupy Surigao Strait, while Kurita would head for the San Bernardino Strait to the north. The U.S. landing force would be caught in a pincer movement between the

Japanese kamikaze pilots preparing for their suicide attacks on U.S. warships.

thousand Japanese lost their lives, as did 1,500 U.S. servicemen. Historians have credited the Japanese, in spite of their loss, with superior strategy and criticized U.S. Admiral William Halsey, in charge of the U.S. forces, for falling for Ozawa's decoy and failing to prevent Kurita from reaching Leyte Gulf.

The U.S. victory allowed MacArthur to land thousands of troops on Leyte. By the end of the year MacArthur was ready to return to Manila, the capital city of the Philippines.

General Tomoyuki Yamashita, Japanese commander in the Philippines, did not plan to fight in Manila. He left about 20,000 troops in the city, in charge of Rear Admiral Iwabuchi, and withdrew northwards to

BATTLE OF LEYTE GULF OCTOBER 24–25, 1944

U.S.:	Fleet carriers	9	Lost 0
Japanese:	Fleet carriers	1	Lost 1
U.S.:	Light carriers	8	Lost 1
Japanese:	Light carriers	3	Lost 3
U.S.:	Escort carriers	29	Lost 2
Japanese:	Escort carriers	0	
U.S.:	Battleships	12	Lost 0
Japanese:	Battleships	9	Lost 3
U.S.:	Heavy cruisers	5	Lost 0
Japanese:	Heavy cruisers	15	Lost 6
U.S.:	Light cruisers	20	Lost 0
Japanese:	Light cruisers	5	Lost 4
U.S.:	Destroyers	162	Lost 4
Japanese:	Destroyers	35	Lost 4

—From *The Second World War in the East*, H.P. Willmott

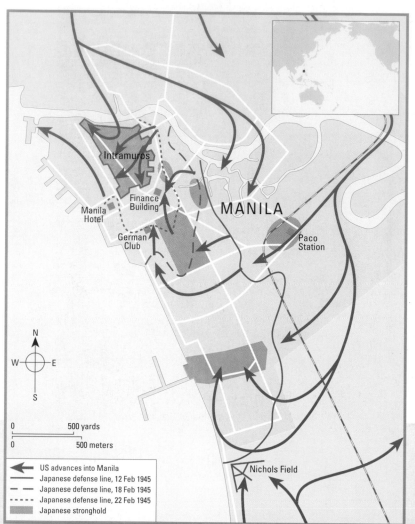

Intramuros

Finance
Building

Manila
Hotel

German
Club

MANILA

Paco
Station

N
W — E
S

0   500 yards
0   500 meters

⬅ US advances into Manila
— — Japanese defense line, 12 Feb 1945
– – – Japanese defense line, 18 Feb 1945
····· Japanese defense line, 22 Feb 1945
▮ Japanese stronghold

Nichols Field

harass the enemy. He even planned to grow his own crops in northern Luzon (*see page 36*) to feed his troops. Iwabuchi, however, chose to avenge his country's disastrous naval defeats by fighting to the bitter end. The resulting fight was the Pacific's only battle in which U.S. and Japanese fought in a city.

Japanese troops stopped the first U.S. advance from the south at Nichols Field, inflicting 900 casualties. A U. S. northern advance turned grim near Paco Station where 300 Japanese held out for two days at a cost of 335 U.S. casualties. On February 15, Iwabuchi rejected Yamashita's order to break out of the city of Manila and made his last stand in Intramuros, a square mile of stone-built buildings surrounded by a high wall.

Left: For every soldier killed in the battle for Manila, which had a population of 800,000, six civilians lost their lives.

A historic moment: General Douglas MacArthur, returning to the Philippines, wades ashore on Leyte on October 25, 1944.

U.S. forces decided to employ heavy artillery and most of the city was reduced to rubble. About 100,000 Filipino residents of the city lost their lives in the fighting, fires, and explosions. The Japanese, believing they were going to die, took to slaughtering civilians, especially European residents. They attacked the German Club, where 1,500 European refugees had taken shelter, killing hundreds of them with bayonets and clubs.

THE COST OF MANILA WAS HIGH

In and around Intramuros, buildings were attacked and destroyed one by one. On February 21, the Manila Hotel was destroyed and four days later, with shells hitting his headquarters, Iwabuchi and others committed suicide. On March 3, the Finance Building, the last building in Japanese hands, was reduced to rubble. The battle for Manila was over.

The United States, which lost 1,100 men, counted over 16,000 Japanese bodies. MacArthur, knowing this cost was too high, ordered that no public monuments commemorating the "liberation" of the city should be erected in either the Philippines or the United States.

The corpse of a U.S. soldier is carried on a stretcher through the ruins of Manila.

WAR TALK

"We are very glad and grateful for the opportunity of being able to serve our country in this epic battle. Now, with what strength remains, we will daringly engage this enemy. Banzai to the Emperor! We are determined to fight to the last man." Vice Admiral Iwabuchi, February 15. 1945.

"People of the Philippines: I have returned. By the grace of Almighty God our forces stand again on Philippine soil—soil consecrated in the blood of our two people . . . Rally to me." General MacArthur, returning to the Philippines two and a half years after he had been forced to leave Corregidor.

—From *Atlas of World War II Battle Plans*, edited by S. Badsey, and *How It Happened: World War II*, edited by Jon E. Lewis

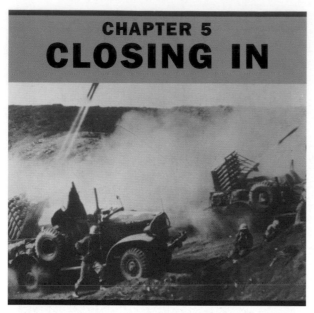

A moment in time: U.S. Marines attack a Japanese position on Iwo Jima, March 23, 1945.

to make it the most heavily fortified island that the U.S. had yet attempted to capture. Mount Suribachi, an extinct volcano at the southern tip of the island, provided cover for defenders firing on the beach. Out of twenty-four U.S. battalion commanders who came ashore in the first landing, nineteen were killed or wounded. The volcanic ash on the beaches could be mixed with cement to make a hard concrete and the defenders used this to reinforce their positions across the island. The Marines fought hard to take the island—their courage is symbolized by the famous photograph taken on February 23 of the American flag being raised on Mount Suribachi.

The human cost of fighting for an island only about five miles (eight km) long was appalling: more than one in three U.S. Marines, nearly 4,000 men, were killed; more than 20,000 Japanese died. The casualty

The Americans' "island hopping" strategy was remarkably successful, and the final objectives in this advance toward Japan were the two islands of Iwo Jima and Okinawa. There were three airfields on Iwo Jima, about 650 miles (1,050 km) south of Tokyo, which could be used to provide fighter cover for long-range B-29 bombers attacking Japan from the Mariana Islands.

Beginning in February 1945, 110,000 U.S. soldiers went ashore on Iwo Jima and some 800 warships became involved in an operation that lasted well over a month. The island's first airfield was taken within forty-eight hours and the second within a week, but the Japanese were securely positioned in the northern part of the island. It was here that the fiercest fighting unfolded.

The geography of Iwo Jima, one of the Volcano Islands, helped

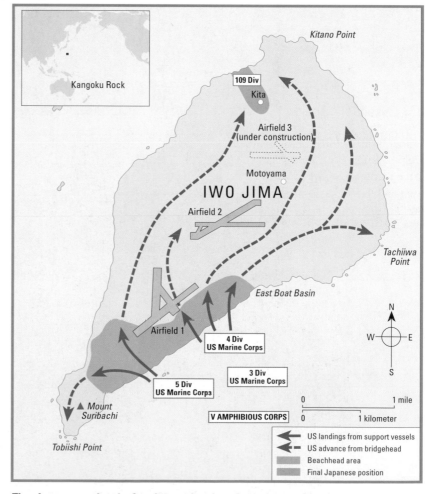

The Japanese dug in for determined resistance against U.S. advances in the north of Iwo Jima.

rate reached 75 percent in two U.S. Marine divisions. Led by Lieutenant General Tadamichi Kuribayashi's very well-organized defense, the Japanese, desperate to keep the enemy from their homeland, fought almost to the last man. In 1956, all American bodies were exhumed and returned to the United States, but

A LETTER HOME

Lieutenant General Kuribayashi and his wife Yoshii had three children. He wrote home regularly, concerned for their welfare: *"Our officers and men know death very well. I am sorry to be fighting the United States of America, but I want to defend this island as long as possible, and to delay the enemy air raids against Tokyo. Ah, you have worked well for a long time as my wife and as a mother of three children. Your life will become harder and more serious. Be careful of your health, and live long. The future of our children will not be easy too. Please take care of them after my death."*

—From *The Battle for Iwo Jima*, Derrick Wright

This famous photograph, showing the U.S. Stars and Stripes being raised on Iwo Jima's Mount Suribachi, symbolizes the determination of the United States to defeat Japan in the Pacific War.

fifty years after the battle, Japanese volunteers were still returning to Iwo Jima to look for the remains of missing soldiers to cremate and return their ashes to Japan.

The island of Okinawa was the final stepping-stone to Japan. The island, about 60 miles (96 km) long, had safe harbors and airfields from which an invasion of Japan could be launched. It was vital for the Japanese to defend it. The United State knew this and mounted its most complex operation in the Pacific War to secure its capture. The Allies had such vast resources that it seemed almost inevitable that Japan would lose the war. Allied naval forces received more oil and gasoline between March and June 1945 than Japan imported in all of 1944. One of the U.S. divisions landed on Okinawa with enough food to supply the city of Colombus, Ohio, for a month. Over half a million troops were involved and more

A wounded Japanese officer emerges from a cave and surrenders on Okinawa.

than 1,200 warships. Carrier-based U.S. aircraft flew more than 90,000 missions during the campaign and the carrier force remained at sea for three months.

The Japanese knew they could not win. The giant *Yamato* battleship and eight destroyers left Japan to fight the Allies with only enough fuel for a one-way voyage. Nearly 2,000 kamikaze missions attacked U.S. ships in waves of massed attacks called *kikusui* (floating chrysanthemums). They inflicted much damage but, in a struggle between U.S. marines fighting to live

A SOLDIER'S NIGHTMARE

In 1984, John Garcia recalled Okinawa. The Japanese woman he refers to was someone he shot in error, mistaking her for a soldier: "*I had friends who were Japanese and I kept thinking every time I pulled a trigger on a man or pushed a flamethrower down into a hole: 'What is this person's family gonna say when he doesn't come back? He's got a wife, he's got children, somebody . . .' I'd get up each day and start drinking. How else could I fight the war? Sometimes we made the booze, sometimes we bought it from the navy . . . Oh, I still lose nights of sleep because of that woman I shot. I still lose a lot of sleep. I still dream about her. I dreamed about it perhaps two weeks ago.*"

—From *"The Good War": An Oral History of World War II*, edited by Studs Terkel

and Japanese pilots dying in order to fight, the the Allied forces captured the island.

ON OKINAWA On Okinawa itself, U.S. forces took three weeks to conquer the Motubo peninsula where the Japanese defenders were concentrated. The other main area of fighting was south of a line between Naha and Yonabaru. On May 27, Naha was fianally in U.S. hands. Out of a garrison force of nearly 80,000 men, only 7,400 Japanese were taken prisoner. Over 7,500 U.S. soldiers died and nearly 5,000 seamen lost their lives on the U.S. side.

The near-suicidal resistance of the Japanese to U.S. advances made the idea of invading Japan itself a fearsome prospect. This bloodiest battle of World War II in the Pacific led to a new policy of bombing Japanese cities, put into effect from March 1945 until the end of the war. It also helped fuel the argument for dropping the atomic bomb, in its very first use, on Japan. Many in the U.S. government hoped that using atomic bombs would stop the war and, in the end, save lives.

Marines of the U.S. 6th Division take cover during the advance on Naha, the capital of Okinawa, where Japanese forces were concentrated.

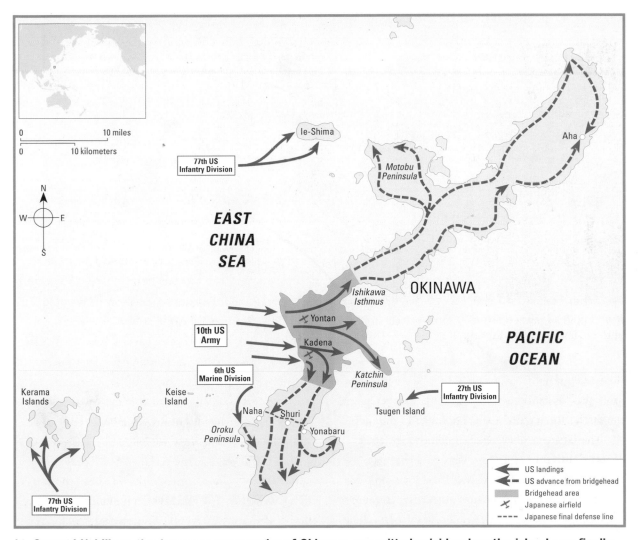

Lt. General Ushijima, the Japanese commander of Okinawa, committed suicide when the island was finally taken by U.S. forces.

SEA OF JAPAN

KOREA

JAPAN

HONSHU

TOKYO

SHIKOKU

KYUSHU

Aomori

Sendai

Nagaoka

Toyama
Utsunomiya
Hitachi
Maebashi
Mito
Kofu
Choshi
Yokohama
Chiba

Nagoya

Kobe
Osaka
Tsu
Sakai
Ujiyamada
Wakayama

Fukui
Hiroshima
Kure
Shimonoseki
Moji
Matsuyama
Yawata
Ube
Fukuoka
Kochi
Sasebo
Uwajima
Omuta
Nagasaki

Miyazaki
Kagoshima
Miyakonojo

| | | 0 | | 100 miles |
| | | 0 | | 100 kilometers |

- ◖ Under 25% of city area destroyed by Allied bombing
- ◗ Between 26–50% area destroyed by Allied bombing
- ◕ Between 51–75% area destroyed by Allied bombing
- ● Over 75% area destroyed by Allied bombing
- ▲ Atomic bomb target

The bombardment of Japan was carried out by almost six hundred U.S. bombers which eventually could attack almost any target they chose, encountering little resistance. The destruction was immense.

Major General Curtis E. LeMay began the bombardment by abandoning the earlier policy of daytime, high-altitude raids that were meant to hit particular targets. These raids were not proving effective, so his new policy involved night raids flying at far lower altitudes. Areas of cities were now subjected to bombing that caused fires rather than explosions. Densely packed Japanese cities had many wooden buildings and fires spread rapidly. All Japanese cities became targets, and about ten million people were killed, injured, or made homeless.

Tokyo, the capital city, suffered especially from firestorms caused by intense bombing. Fires consumed more and more oxygen, turning the city into one large inferno, with temperatures rising to 1,472° F (800° C), fanned by hurricane force winds. In one raid on March 9, eighty-three thousand civilians died.

REDUCED TO RUINS Between mid-May and mid-June, B-29 bombers reduced six of Japan's major industrial cities close to ruins. Protected by fighters from Iwo Jima, these huge aircraft also

Men load bombs onto one of the 3,970 Superfortress B-29 bombers built by the U.S. for use only in the Pacific War. The aircraft was based on Saipan Island, in the Mariana Islands.

bombed during the day. They shot down so many Japanese fighters trying to hit the B-29s that the Japanese grounded their remaining aircraft, keeping them for use against the expected land invasion. By August, Japan's economy had been largely disabled by the bombing raids and over a quarter of a million civilians had been killed. Most Japanese now realized that their country could not win the war, but military leaders insisted that further resistance would force the United States to negotiate a peace that was better for Japan.

"BLOWN AWAY"

Schoolgirl Funato Kazuyo, with her two brothers, Kōichi and Minoru, and her younger sister, Hiroko, were in a shelter [in Tokyo] when they realized a fire was heading towards them: *"When we went out, we could see to the west, in the direction of Fukagawa, everything was bright red. The north wind was incredibly strong. The drone of the planes was an overwhelming roar, shaking earth and sky. Everywhere, incendiary bombs were falling. . . . . [They ran from the fire and took shelter elsewhere] "We lay flat on our stomachs, thinking we would be all right if the fire was gone by morning, but the fire kept pelting down on us. Minoru suddenly let out a horrible scream and leapt out of the shelter, flames shooting out of his back. Kōichi stood up calling, 'Minoru!' and instantly, he too, was blown away. Only Hiroko and I remained."*

—From *Japan At War,* Haruko Taya Cook and Theodore F. Cook

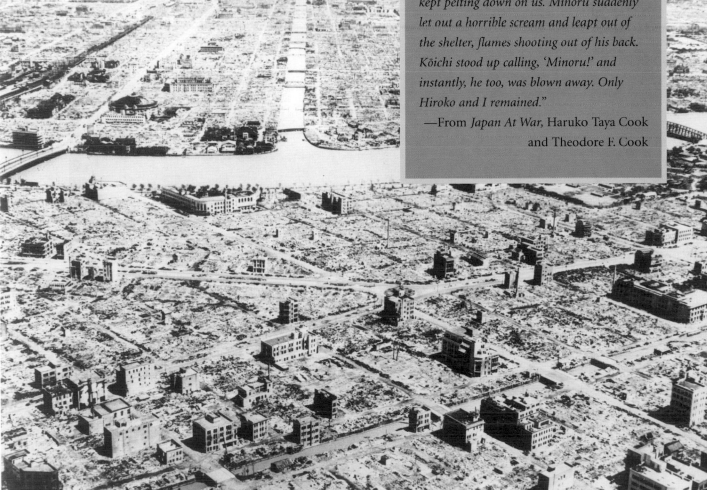

Nearly half of the entire urban area of Tokyo was flattened by U.S. bombing raids between March and June 1945, and still, Japan would not surrender.

World War II was drawing to a close. Nazi Germany had surrendered to the Allies in May 1945, and the U.S. advance toward Japan was reaching a climax. Meanwhile, war still raged in another, less well-known theater in China and Burma (Myanmar).

CHIANG KAI-SHEK

Chinese nationalists under Chiang Kai-shek, who had been fighting Japanese forces since the invasion in 1937, were supported by the Allies and supplied with arms and money. The Japanese invasion of Burma early in 1942 cut off the supply line to the nationalists, and fighting developed for the control of Burma. The turning point in this war came in March 1944 when Allied troops, mostly Indians under the British General William Slim, were attacked by the Japanese at Imphal in India.

The opposing armies battled it out for months, but the Japanese were gradually worn down, and by July they were forced to withdraw. General Slim pushed into Burma and captured Mandalay and then Burma's capital city, Rangoon.

The success of the U.S. "island hopping" strategy in the Pacific made the fate of Burma less important to the Allies. The Allies also began to think that Chiang Kai-shek was not an effective ally. It was his communist rival, Mao Zedong, who was more useful in helping to tie up about a million Japanese troops in China.

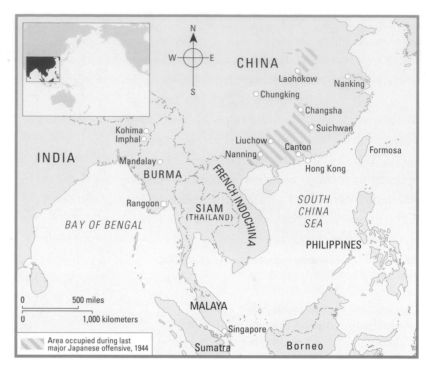

Above: Fighting in China tied up about one million Japanese soldiers and helped Mao Zedong and his Communist army emerge as the future face of the country. The map shows the area occupied during Japan's last major offensive in China in 1944.

Mao Zedong addresses a crowd in November 1944. The war against Japan helped bring about, in 1949, the creation of the People's Republic of China, a communist nation.

The success of Chinese troops against the Japanese, under the command of the U.S. General Joseph Stilwell, only confirmed Chiang Kai-shek's ineffectiveness. Both Stilwell and Chiang Kai-shek were supplied from India, with U.S. and British pilots flying over a series of mountain ridges, nicknamed the Hump, to make the supply drops. The awful human cost of China's fight against Japan often tends to be forgotten by countries outside of Asia and in many accounts of World War II. The number of Chinese nationalists who died fighting and civilians who died through starvation and disease is impossible to calculate, but it certainly reaches into the millions.

General Slim's Fourteenth Army, composed of British, Indian, Burmese, Chinese, and African soldiers, advances toward Mandalay, Burma, in March 1945.

" . . . FOR MY MOTHERLAND!"

Uno Shintaro, fighting in China, recalls a young Chinese prisoner called Cheng Jing who was proved to have stolen some guns: "*...He was only sixteen or seventeen. He looked so innocent and naïve that they brought him back without killing him. He soon learned our Japanese songs and some officers put him to work in the regimental armoury repairing weapons. Everyone trusted him. The regiment received twenty to thirty pistols each year. That year they went missing. Cheng Jing had stolen them and passed them along to the guerrillas . . . When he realized he wouldn't be spared, his attitude changed . . . As Cheng Jing passed by the door of my room on the way to his execution, he shouted at me, 'I will avenge myself on you! I did it for my motherland!'*"

—From *Japan at War*, Haruko Taya Cook and Theodore F. Cook

Left: The city of Hiroshima flattened to the ground as the result of a single atomic bomb.

Below: A mushroom cloud over Nagasaki, a result of the atom bomb dropped on the city: 'When you deal with a beast you have to treat him as a beast,' wrote President Truman after the attack.

In the full context of World War II, the possibility that Nazi Germany would develop an atomic bomb led the United States to develop its own weapon of mass destruction. When it was ready, the new bomb was used against Japan instead. Plans for the invasion of Japan, with its anticipated high costs in life, supplies, and money, were no longer needed once the atomic bombs had been dropped on the cities of Hiroshima (August 6) and Nagasaki (August 9). On August 14, Japan's Emperor Hirohito finally announced on Japanese radio that their country had been defeated. Japan surrendered, bringing the Pacific War and World War II to an end.

The use of the atomic bomb remains one of the most controversial issue of the war, although it aroused no great public disagreement in 1945. The long-term consequences of dropping the atom bomb, however, were profound. The world was now changed into a planet where nuclear weapons could destroy civilizations and damage the world's ecology. Some of the scientists involved in the development of the atom bomb realized this and did not want the new weapon to be used. They were overruled because the need to defeat the Japanese was seen the most important concern.

HARRY S. TRUMAN Harry S. Truman, the president of the United States at the time, had been informed that between 25,000 and 46,000 Americans

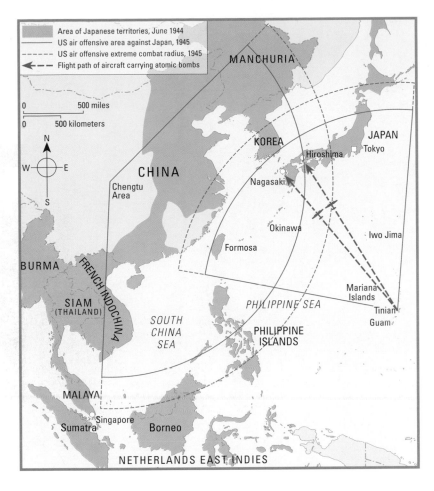

Area of Japanese territories, June 1944
US air offensive area against Japan, 1945
US air offensive extreme combat radius, 1945
Flight path of aircraft carrying atomic bombs

MANCHURIA

0 — 500 miles
0 — 500 kilometers

N
W E
S

KOREA   JAPAN

CHINA   Hiroshima   Tokyo

Chengtu   Nagasaki
Area

Okinawa   Iwo Jima

Formosa

BURMA   FRENCH INDOCHINA

SIAM   Mariana
(THAILAND)   SOUTH   Islands
              CHINA   PHILIPPINE SEA   Tinian
              SEA   PHILIPPINE   Guam
                         ISLANDS

MALAYA

Singapore
Sumatra   Borneo

NETHERLANDS EAST INDIES

ATOMIC BOMBS: THE FACTS

Date:	August 6, 1945
Time:	8:15 A.M.
Target of atomic bomb:	Hiroshima, population: 350,000
Type of atomic bomb:	Uranium
Bomb's nickname:	"Little Boy"
Length of bomb:	9.8 feet (3 m)
People killed:	140,000
Date:	August 9, 1945
Time:	11:02 A.M.
Target of atomic bomb:	Nagasaki, population: 70,000
Type of atomic bomb:	Plutonium
Bomb's nickname:	"Fat Man"
Length of bomb:	11.5 feet (3.5 m)
People killed:	73,884

From Tinian, one of the Mariana Islands captured in 1944, B-29 bombers took off carrying atomic bombs to drop on Hiroshima and Nagasaki in August 1945.

were likely to die in an invasion of Japan. It is argued to this day that these lives, and those of many Japanese, were saved by the use of the bomb. Others argue that lives could have been saved on both sides if surrender terms had been negotiated before using the bomb. Japanese military leaders knew their country was defeated and peace negotiations had already begun. Settlement was prevented by Japan's fear that their Emperor, regarded as a god at the time, would be dethroned if Japan surrendered unconditionally. If it had been agreed that the Emperor could continue to rule, as he was actually allowed to do after 1945, then a negotiated surrender might have taken place. Some historians believe that the U.S. feared a confrontation with the Union of Soviet Socialist Republics (USSR), and that using the new weapon was intended to help the U.S. keep the USSR at bay in what soon became the Cold War.

When the Pacific War was over, a tribunal was set up in Tokyo to punish those found guilty of war crimes. Twenty-five Japanese leaders were tried and sentenced to long terms of imprisonment or to execution. About 3,000 other individuals were found guilty in other war crimes trials that took place in the Pacific region, and 920 were executed. Emperor Hirohito

Officials representing the Japanese government arrive on the battleship USS *Missouri* to sign surrender terms on September 2, 1945; the Pacific War was finally over.

and many members of his family were granted immunity because the United States wanted to avoid the widespread opposition to their occupation of Japan that Hirohito's trial would have created. This decision has been criticized by some, as has the fact that those running the trials all came from countries that had suffered at the hands of Japan in the war. One of the judges (there were no juries) was a survivor of the Bataan death march and could hardly be impartial.

The long-term consequences of World War II in the Pacific were huge. In China, civil war between Chiang Kai-shek's forces and communists under Mao Zedong led in 1949 to the creation of the Communist People's Republic of China. In the last week of the war, the USSR declared war on Japan, as the Allies had earlier agreed, and invaded northern Korea. This led to an agreed division of Korea, with the north under the influence of the USSR and the south under

U.S. influence. Within five years of the end of World War II, hostilities erupted between North and South Korea, and the country became a major theater of conflict in the Cold War.

Perhaps the most important long-term consequence of the Pacific War was that it ended the supremacy of European colonial powers in Asia. In Vietnam, nationalist and communist forces opposing the Japanese were unwilling to accept the return of their French colonial masters. The French eventually withdrew, setting the stage for U.S. anti-communist intervention and the Vietnam War. The Dutch also gave up any attempt to retain their colonial possessions and the state of Indonesia emerged. India, Burma, Malaya and Singapore also struggled and negotiated to gain their independence from Britain. The map of Asia had changed and the U.S. emerged as the major power in the Pacific.

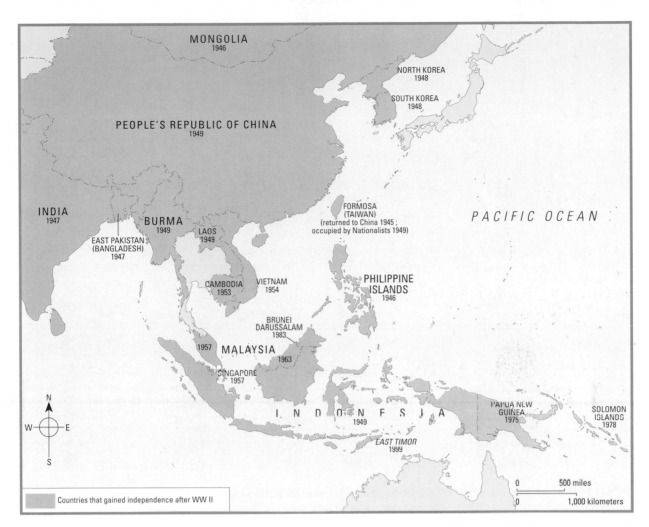

MONGOLIA
1946

NORTH KOREA
1948

SOUTH KOREA
1948

PEOPLE'S REPUBLIC OF CHINA
1949

INDIA
1947

BURMA
1949

LAOS
1949

EAST PAKISTAN
(BANGLADESH)
1947

FORMOSA
(TAIWAN)
(returned to China 1945;
occupied by Nationalists 1949)

PACIFIC OCEAN

CAMBODIA
1953

VIETNAM
1954

PHILIPPINE
ISLANDS
1946

BRUNEI
DARUSSALAM
1983

1957

MALAYSIA
1963

SINGAPORE
1957

INDONESIA
1949

PAPUA NEW
GUINEA
1975

SOLOMON
ISLANDS
1978

EAST TIMOR
1999

N
W E
S

0   500 miles
0   1,000 kilometers

Countries that gained independence after WW II

Many countries in East Asia gained independence after the war. Comparing this map with the one on page 5 shows some of the important changes brought about by World War II in the Pacific.

"WAR IS TERRIBLE"

Richard Kennard, a U.S. Marine who fought in the Pacific War, ended a letter home with this thought:

"War is terrible, just awful, awful. You have no idea ... After this is all over, I shall cherish and respect more than anything else all that which is sweet, tender and gentle.

Much love to you all

(Your son and Lynn's sweetheart)

Dick"

—Quoted in *How It Happened: World War II*, edited by Jon E. Lewis

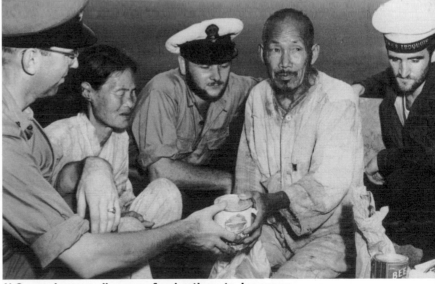

U.S. servicemen dispense food rations to Japanese civilians at the end of World War II in the Pacific.

PROFILES OF MILITARY AND POLITICAL LEADERS

CHIANG KAI-SHEK
(1887–1975)
Leader of Chinese nationalists fighting the Japanese after their invasion of China. He was opposed by Mao Zedong, the leader of Communist nationalists who were also fighting the Japanese. Chiang Kai-shek was defeated in the civil war that resumed between the two sides after 1945.

WINSTON SPENCER CHURCHILL

(1874–1965)
Prime Minister of Great Britain 1940–45. Churchill had to accept U.S. leadership in the conduct of the Pacific War, especially after the surrender of British land forces to the Japanese in Singapore. Churchill was a strong supporter of the colonialist policies of his country's empire. He hoped to restore British influence in southeast Asia after the war and maintain the British empire. In this goal, he was not successful.

ADMIRAL WILLIAM HALSEY
(1882–1959)
U.S. Commander, Aircraft, Battle Force Pacific. When the Japanese attacked Pearl Harbor, Halsey's ability and willingness to take the offensive contributed to the success of the Guadalcanal campaign, which led to his promotion. Admired for his tough approach, he was appointed Commander South Pacific and South Pacific Area by General Nimitz.

HIROHITO (1901–1989)
Emperor of Japan from 1926 until his death. There is controversy regarding Hirohito's degree of responsibility for bringing Japan into the war. In 1945, many people regarded him as a war leader  who ought to be put on trial and punished. The fact that he was not prosecuted after the war is something that still causes dissent. Evidence suggests that he opposed the military leaders in 1941 but could not prevent them from pursuing the aggressive policy that led to the attack on Pearl Harbor. Hirohito played an important role in bringing about the surrender of Japan in 1945.

LIEUTENANT GENERAL MASAHARU HOMMA
(1887–1946)
Japanese army officer who captured the Philippines from the forces of Douglas MacArthur. The campaign took longer than had been planned and Homma was recalled to Japan in August 1942. He remained unemployed for the rest of the war but in 1946 he was tried for war crimes committed by his soldiers. Homma claimed that he was unaware of what had happened on the Bataan death march but he was found guilty and executed.

MAJOR GENERAL CURTIS E. LEMAY (1906–1990)
One of the younger U.S. generals, largely responsible for the air offensive against Japan in 1945. He abandoned the tactic of high-level precision air attacks in favor of low-level incendiary bombing, which led to violent fires across entire cities and a masssive number of civilian deaths.

GENERAL DOUGLAS MACARTHUR (1880–1964)
Supreme Allied Commander of the South West Pacific Command during the Pacific War. A controversial leader, MacArthur historians regard him as very fortunate to have escaped blame for the defense of the Philippines that resulted in the U.S. defeat. When ordered to escape to Australia in 1942, he famously declared "I shall return," refusing  the U.S. Office of War Information suggestion that he should change the phrase to "We shall return." MacArthur, very effective in "island-hopping" to bypass pockets of strong Japanese resistance, recaptured the Philippines in 1944. If a land invasion of Japan had been necessary, MacArthur would have been the ground commander for the operation. In the Korean War, MacArthur successfully led the U.S. forces, but President Truman fired him when he tried to continue the war into China.

MAO ZEDONG

(1893–1976)
A founding member of the Chinese Communist Party in 1921, Mao had risen to lead the Party by the time of the Pacific War. He effectively opposed Chiang Kai-shek by dealing with corruption and social issues and gained support as a nationalist by fighting the Japanese. By 1945, Mao and his troops had gained control over most of the Chinese countryside. Four years later, he declared the independence of the People's Republic of China.

ADMIRAL CHESTER W. NIMITZ (1885–1966)

Commander-in-Chief U.S. Pacific Fleet and Pacific Ocean Areas during the Pacific War. He was overshadowed to some extent by the more flamboyant MacArthur, though he is regarded as possessing far sounder military judgment. Nimitz planned the Battle of Midway and chose to act on valuable information provided by U.S. intelligence that deciphered Japanese radio messages. Nimitz commanded the landings on Iwo Jima and Okinawa, and signed the Japanese surrender document on behalf of the United States.

FRANKLIN D. ROOSEVELT (1882–1945)

President of the United States at the time of the attack on Pearl Harbor, Roosevelt died in April 1945 and so did not live to see the surrender of Japan. Roosevelt is credited for his leadership in uniting his country in the war against Nazi Germany and Japan. Historians have recognized Roosevelt's ability to manage the two separate wars within World War II successfully: one in Europe and one in the Pacific. Roosevelt is also thought to have realized that relations with the USSR would be difficult once the war was over.

GENERAL SIR WILLIAM SLIM (1891–1970)

British commander in charge of the 1944 defense of Imphal, India, and of the campaign that drove the Japanese from Burma in 1945. He once said "I must have been the most defeated

general in our history," but historians have given him great credit for his tactics and his ability to command troops and win the loyalty of soldiers.

ADMIRAL RAYMOND A. SPRUANCE (1886–1969)

A commander at the battle of Midway, Spruance took part in the battle of the Philippine Sea, the Okinawa campaign, and also planned the capture of Tarawa and the Marshall islands. The U.S. Navy's official historian praised his "power of decision and coolness in action."

GENERAL JOSEPH STILWELL (1883–1946)

A U.S. army commander in the China-Burma-India theater of war who became well known for his harsh criticisms of Chiang Kai-shek. Stilwell, who spoke Chinese fluently, was very successful as a commander of Chinese troops. He gained admiration and promotion for the way he handled his troops and conducted a difficult campaign. Stilwell was also renowned for his inability to get along with British military commanders.

GENERAL HIDEKI TOJO (1884–1948)

Prime Minister of Japan between 1941 and 1944, he ordered the attack on Pearl Harbor. Before 1941, Tojo was known for his hard-line attitude toward the U.S. and his willingness to use military solutions for political problems. Tojo supported Nazi Germany and, after the war, was convicted of war crimes and hanged.

HARRY S. TRUMAN (1884–1972)

Vice President of the United States for 83 days, until the death of Roosevelt in April 1945 made Truman the President. As Vice President, he had not known about the program to build atomic

weapons but, guided by Roosevelt's advisers after Japan refused to surrender, he ordered that atomic bombs be dropped on Hiroshima and Nagasaki.

ADMIRAL ISOROKU YAMAMOTO (1884–1943)

Commander of the Japanese Combined Fleet, 1939–43. Yamamoto had lived and studied in the United States and, in the 1930s, was opposed to people like Tojo who favored war with the U. S. When the prospect of war loomed, however, Yamamoto felt that only a surprise attack on Pearl Harbor would give his country hope of success, so he worked out the plan for attacking the U.S. fleet. He also planned the strategy that led to the Battle of Midway. Yamamoto was killed by U.S. forces when his aircraft was shot down.

GENERAL TOMOYUKI YAMASHITA (1885–1946)

Commander of Japanese forces that conquered Malaya and Singapore, and the commander responsible for the defense of Luzon in the Philippines. After the war, he was put on trial for war crimes committed against civilians in Manila. Yamashita was not directly responsible for these crimes but he was found guilty and sentenced to death. MacArthur refused to consider his appeal and Yamashita was hanged.

TIME LINE

SEPTEMBER 1931
Japan invades Manchuria, China.

AUGUST 1937
Japan further invades China.

SEPTEMBER 1, 1939
Nazi Germany invades Poland.

SEPTEMBER 3, 1939
Britain, France, Australia, and India declare war on Nazi Germany.

MAY 15, 1940
Dutch (Netherlands) army surrenders to Nazi Germany.

JULY 24, 1941
Japanese troops begin occupation of French-controlled Indochina.

JULY 26, 1941
U.S. freezes all Japanese assets.

AUGUST 1, 1941
U.S. begins oil embargo against Japan; British and Dutch soon join.

DECEMBER 7–8, 1941
Japanese troops land in Malaya and Siam. Japan attacks Pearl Harbor, forcing U.S. into World War II.

DECEMBER 9, 1941
Australia and New Zealand declare war on Japan.

DECEMBER 10, 1941
HMS *Prince of Wales* and *Repulse* are sunk off coast of Malaya. Japan lands troops in Philippines.

DECEMBER 11, 1941
Nazi Germany and fascist Italy declare war on the United States.

DECEMBER 14, 1941
Japan begins invasion of Burma.

DECEMBER 17 and 20, 1941
Japan invades North Borneo and then the Netherlands East Indies.

DECEMBER 25, 1941
Japan invades and captures Hong Kong.

JANUARY 9, 1942
Following the capture of Manila by Japan, the siege of Bataan begins.

JANUARY 23, 1942
Japanese land on Solomon Islands.

JANUARY 25, 1942
British-led forces in Malaya ordered to withdraw to island of Singapore.

FEBRUARY 15, 1942
British surrender Singapore to Japan.

MARCH 7, 1942
Japanese land in New Guinea.

MARCH 11, 1942
General MacArthur leaves Philippines for Australia.

APRIL 7, 1942
U.S. and Filipino troops surrender on Bataan; "Death March" follows.

APRIL 18, 1942
Sixteen USAAF B-25 bombers (launched from the USS *Hornet* off the coast of Japan) bomb Tokyo and other Japanese cities.

MAY 6, 1942
Corregidor island falls to Japan.

MAY 7–8, 1942
Battle of the Coral Sea slows Japan.

JUNE 4–5, 1942
Battle of Midway is Japan's first defeat in the Pacific.

AUGUST 7–8, 1942
First U.S. landings on Guadalcanal. Battle of Savo Island helps Japan.

SEPTEMBER 27, 1942
Japan's advance on Port Moresby is halted.

NOVEMBER 12–13, 1942
Naval battle of Guadalcanal begins.

JANUARY 21, 1943
Japanese base at Gona, New Guinea, captured; Sanananda Point cleared.

FEBRUARY 9, 1943
Last Japanese troops begin to leave Guadalcanal.

JUNE 20, 1943
U.S. troops land on New Georgia.

AUGUST 15, 1943
U.S. troops land on Vella Lavella.

OCTOBER 6–7, 1943
Japanese evacuate Vella Lavella.

NOVEMBER 20, 1943
U.S. landings on Tarawa and Bougainville.

JANUARY 30, 1944
U.S. landings on Marshall Islands.

FEBRUARY 17, 1944
Eniwetok Atoll attacked and secured by U.S. forces.

MARCH 8, 1944
Japan's offensive from Burma into India begins.

APRIL 22, 1944
MacArthur's forces land in New Guinea.

JUNE 15, 1944
Americans land on Saipan and begin Strategic bombing campaign.

JUNE 19, 1944
Battle of the Philippine Sea wages the war's biggest carrier fight.

JULY 9, 1944
Saipan secured by U.S. forces.

JULY 18, 1944
Japan defeated at Imphal, India.

JULY 21–24, 1944
U.S. landings on Guam and Tinian.

SEPTEMBER 15, 1944
U.S. forces land on Peleliu.

OCTOBER 24, 1944
U.S. landings at Leyte, Philippines. Battle of Leyte Gulf.

JANUARY 9, 1945
U.S. forces land on Luzon.

FEBRUARY 1945
Battle for Manila begins.

FEBRUARY 19, 1945
U.S. forces land on Iwo Jima.

MARCH 3, 1945
MacArthur's U.S. forces capture Manila.

MARCH 9, 1945
First firebomb attack on Tokyo.

MARCH 20, 1945
British-led troops secure Mandalay, Burma.

MARCH 26, 1945
Fighting ends on Iwo Jima.

APRIL 1, 1945
U.S. troops land on Okinawa.

APRIL 12, 1945
Truman becomes president after the death of President Roosevelt.

MAY 3, 1945
Allied troops capture Rangoon, Burma.

AUGUST 6, 1945
U.S. drops atomic bomb on the Japanese city of Hiroshima.

AUGUST 8, 1945
USSR declares war on Japan.

AUGUST 9, 1945
U.S. drops atomic bomb on the Japanese city of Nagasaki.

AUGUST 14, 1945
Japanese emperor radio broadcasts to the country, accepting surrender.

SEPTEMBER 2, 1945
Formal surrender of Japan signed aboard the USS *Missouri*, in Tokyo Bay.

MAY 3, 1946
Tokyo war crimes tribunal begins.

AUGUST 14–15, 1947
India becomes independent from Britain.

JUNE 12, 1948
Armed struggle against the British in Malaya for independence.

OCTOBER 1, 1949
Mao Zedong declares Communist People's Republic of China.

DECEMBER 31, 1949
The Dutch formally surrender control over Indonesia.

SEPTEMBER 1951
U.S.-led occupation of Japan ends.

Casualties in the Pacific

Australia: Over 17,000 deaths; 14,000 wounded.

China: An estimated 5 million military casualties (killed and wounded); civilian casualties estimated between 10 and 20 million.

India: Over 24,000 deaths in military action; an estimated three million civilian deaths as a result of war-related famine in 1943.

Great Britain: 30,000 deaths; number of wounded unknown.

Japan: 1.8 million deaths in military action; 500,000 civilians killed.

United States: 80,000 deaths; number of wounded unknown.

It is difficult to estimate the number of civilians killed in the course of the war but in total many millions, in the Netherlands East Indies, the Pacific Islands, the Philippines, Burma, Malaya and Korea, died as a result of Japanese occupation and military engagements in their countries.

Combatant Nations

Australia: After Pearl Harbor and the invasion of Malaya, Australia declared war on Japan in December 1941.

China: Invaded by Japanese in 1937, although the Chinese region of Manchuria had been invaded six years earlier. The China Incident, as the Japanese called their fighting there, became part of the Pacific War, and part of World War II as a whole, after Japan attacked the U.S. at Pearl Harbor in 1941.

Great Britain: Britain and Japan were at war after the Japanese invasion of Malaya in 1941. Britain was already a combatant nation in World War II, having declared war on Nazi Germany in September 1939.

Japan: Japan was at war with China from 1937. After Japan both attacked Pearl Harbor and invaded the British colony of Malaya at the end of 1941, Japan was at war with the U.S. and Britain.

United States: Japan and the United States were at war after Japan attacked Pearl Harbor in December 1941.

U.S. Warships Completed or Obtained between July 1940 and September 1945

Battleships	10
Aircraft carriers	27
Escort carriers	111
Cruisers	47
Destroyers	370
Destroyer escorts	504
Submarines	217
Minecraft	975
Patrol ships and craft	1,915
Auxiliary ships	1,612
Landing ships and craft	66,055

Japanese Naval Strength on December 7, 1941

	Existing strength	Under construction
Battleships	10	2
Aircraft carriers	10	4
Cruisers	38	4
Destroyers	112	12
Submarines	65	29
Others	156	88

Comparison of Japanese and U.S. Military Production Figures

	1939	1940	1941	1942	1943	1944	1945
Aircraft, U.S.	5,856	12,804	26,277	47,836	85,898	96,318	49,761
Aircraft, Japan	4,467	4,768	5,088	8,861	16,693	28,180	11,066
Tanks, U.S.	–	400	4,052	24,997	29,497	17,565	11,968
Tanks, Japan	–	1,023	1,024	1,191	790	401	142
Major naval vessels, U.S.	–	–	544	1,854	2,654	2,247	1,513
Major naval vessels, Japan	21	30	49	68	122	248	51

Pacific War Crimes Trials: Verdicts and Sentences

Count	1	27	29	31	32	33	35	36	54	55	Sentence
Araki Sadao	G	G	A	A	A	A	A	A	A	A	Life imprisonment
Doihara Kenjiō	G	G	G	G	G	A	G	G	G	O	Hanging
Hashimoto Kingorō	G	G	A	A	A				A	A	Life imprisonment
Hata Shunroku	G	G	G	G	G	A	A	G	A	A	Life imprisonment
Hiranuma Kiichirō	G	G	G	G	G	A	A	G	A	A	Hanging
Hirota Kōki	G	G	A	A	A	A	A		A	G	Life imprisonment
Hoshino Naoki	G	G	G	G	G	A	A		A	A	Life imprisonment
Itagaki Seishirō	G	G	G	G	G	A	G	G	G	O	Hanging
Kaya Okinori	G	G	G	G	G				A	A	Life imprisonment
Kido Koichi	G	G	G	G	G	A	A	A	A	A	Life imprisonment
Kimura Heitarō	G	G	G	G	G				G	G	Hanging
Koiso Kuniaki	G	G	G	G	G			A	A	G	Life imprisonment
Matsui Iwane	A	A	A	A	A		A	A	A	G	Hanging
Minami Jirō	G	G	A	A	A				A	A	Life imprisonment
Mutō Akira	G	G	G	G	G	A		A	G	G	Hanging
Oka Takasumi	G	G	G	G	G				A	A	Life imprisonment
Oshima Hiroshi	G	A	A	A	A				A	A	Life imprisonment
Satō Kenryō	G	G	G	G	G				A	A	Life imprisonment
Shigemitsu Mamoru	A	G	G	G	G	G	A		A	G	7 years imprisonment
Shiimada Shigetarō	G	G	G	G	G						Life imprisonment
Shiratori Toshio	G	A	A	A	A						Life imprisonment
Suzuki Teiichi	G	G	G	G	G		A	A	A	A	Life imprisonment
Tōgō Shigenori	G	G	G	G	G			A	A	A	20 years imprisonment
Tōjō Hideki	G	G	G	G	G	G		A	G	O	Hanging
Umezo Yoshijirō	G	G	G	G	G	G		A	A	A	Life imprisonment

Key

Blank: Not accused of this count. G: Guilty. A: Acquitted (not guilty). O: Charged but no verdict reached.

Count 1: Overall conspiracy to wage war against "international law, treaties, agreements or assurances"
Count 27: Waging war against China
Count 29: Waging war against the United States
Count 31: Waging war against the British Commonwealth
Count 32: Waging war against the Netherlands
Count 33: Waging war against France
Count 35: Waging war against the USSR at Lake Khassan
Count 36: Waging war against the USSR at Nomonhan
Count 54: Ordering, authorizing, or permitting atrocities
Count 55: Disregard of duty to secure observance of and prevent breaches of Laws of War

GLOSSARY

aircraft carrier A large ship with a flight deck from which aircraft may take off and land.

Allies The countries at war against Germany, Italy, Japan and their supporters.

atoll A ridge of coral rock and sand, rising just above sea level, enclosing an area of sea.

banzai A form of greeting, traditionally used by the Japanese to their emperor. A term also used to describe an open, near-suicidal charge by Japanese soldiers against an enemy.

battalion A military formation, made up of an average of around 750 men and under the command of a Lieutenant Colonel.

battleship The largest and most heavily-armed type of warship.

campaign A series of military operations in a particular theater of war.

civilians People who are not part of the armed forces of a navy, army, or air force.

Cold War The period of international tension between 1945 and 1991 when a high level of distrust existed between the U.S. and the USSR.

colonial Relating to a colony.

colony A country whose native population is denied true self-rule; ruled and inhabited by people who represent a foreign government.

conscripted Forced to join armed services.

convoy A group of merchant ships (or other vehicles) travelling together for mutual protection.

cruiser A warship that is less heavily armed than a battleship but which has greater speed.

destroyer A warship used to attack enemy shipping with torpedoes and to protect its own fleet from attack by warships and submarines.

division A military formation made up of an average of about 12,000 men; Japanese divisions were as large as 18,000 under a single command.

emplacement A platform for guns.

evacuate Withdraw from a place, such as the scene of battle, often because the situation is considered too dangerous.

exhume Dig up, unearth, especially the dead.

Filipinos People native to the Philippines.

garrison A fortified position in which troops and their equipment are stationed.

guerrillas Independent fighters who are not part of a regular government army but who conduct military action.

hypocrites People who say one thing but do another.

immunity Freedom from the normal consequences of a law.

impartial Fair, not favoring one side or another in a dispute.

imperialism A belief in the value of acquiring control over another country's resources and the establishment of colonies, often considered part of the controlling country's empire.

imports Goods brought into a country or a region from other countries.

incendiary bombs Bombs designed to create fires rather than to explode.

Indochina A region of southeast Asia, including modern Vietnam, which was a colony of France before World War II.

intelligence In a military sense, the collecting of information about the enemy.

interned Placed under a form of imprisonment whereby people are guarded and restricted to one place.

kamikaze Japanese suicide pilots who undertook missions against enemy ships.

killing zone An area where a concentrated amount of killing in the course of a battle takes place.

liberators People who free others from a state of captivity or political oppression.

Malaya Country in Asia, now called Malaysia, which was a British colony in 1941 when it was overrun by the Japanese.

Manchuria A Chinese state, a territory once disputed by China, Japan, and the Soviet Union, occupied by the Japanese in 1931.

marines Soldiers based on warships. Marines typically take part in amphibious operations, landing by sea to engage enemy forces on land.

medic Someone who provides medical care.

Mount Niitaka The highest mountain in Japan, the name of which was used as a code for the attack on Pearl Harbor in 1941.

nationalists People who hold strong patriotic beliefs and who are very loyal to the nation to which they belong.

natural resources Sources of food and fuel, such as wheat or oil for example, that belong to a country or region.

Nazi Germany Germany, between 1933 and 1945, when the country was governed by Adolf Hitler and members of the Nazi party.

Netherlands (Holland) Country of the Dutch people in western Europe that lost control over its colonies in Asia after being defeated by Germany in 1940.

Netherlands East Indies Dutch colony in southeast Asia that became Indonesia when it achieved independence after World War II.

peninsula A piece of land surrounded by water on three sides.

Philippines A Pacific archipelago off southeast Asia made up of thousands of islands. It had a population of 17 million in 1941, and was an American colony but was on its way to achieving independence when the Pacific War broke out.

pincer movement An encircling movement that closes in on the enemy.

Siam Now the independent nation of Thailand, this country in Asia was invaded by the Japanese in 1941.

siege A military tactic that forces a group to surrender by surrounding them and preventing food and support from reaching them.

strategy A plan for the way military forces and resources are used in a military campaign.

supply lines Routes used to provide supplies and weapons during a war.

tactics The plan for the best way to achieve the aims of military strategy by using military forces when they are in actual contact with the enemy.

task force A unit of people and equipment organized for a special purpose.

theater of war A large geographical area where a series of major battles occur.

traumatic Describes an event that brings about a state of deep emotional shock.

tribunal A court of justice.

unconditional surrender A complete surrender of forces without any question or protest, and before any prior agreement, conditions, or terms of peace have been established.

USSR The Union of Soviet Socialist Republics (also known as the Soviet Union), of which Russia was the leading power. It was disbanded at the end of 1991.

RECOMMENDED BOOKS

The following books look at the Pacific War as a whole or at some of the key episodes in the Pacific War:

Chrisp, Peter. *The World Wars: The War in The Pacific.* Raintree/Steck Vaughn, 2004.

Denenberg, Barry. *Early Sunday Morning: The Pearl Harbor Diary of Amber Billows, Hawaii, 1941.* Scholastic, 2003.

Earle, Jr. Rice. *Strategic Battles in the Pacific: World War II.* Lucent Books, 2000.

Grant, R.G. *Hiroshima and Nagasaki.* Hodder and Stoughton Children's Division, 1999.

Klam, Julie and Dwight Jon Zimmerman. *Victory in the Pacific.* Smart Apple Media, 2003.

Stein, R. Conrad. *World War II in the Pacific.* Enslow Publishers, Inc., 2001.

Tames, Richard. *Turning Points in History: Pearl Harbor.* Heineman Educational Books, Library Division, 2000.

Nardo, Don. *World War II in the Pacific (*World History Series*).* Lucent Books, 2002

Yep, Laurence. *Hiroshima.* Apple, 1996.

The following books provide interesting, detailed accounts of Pacific War battles or campaigns:

Badsey, Stephen, ed. *The Hutchison Atlas of World War II Battle Plans.* Helicon, 2000.

Fuchida, Okumiya, Mitsuo, and Okumiyo, Masatake. *Midway: The Japanese Story.* United States Naval Institute, 2001.

Grove, Eric. *Sea Battles in Close-Up: World War 2,* Specialist Marketing International, 1988.

Leasor, James. *Singapore: The Battle That Changed The War,* 2001.

Moran, Jim and Gordon L.Rottman. *Peleliu, 1944: The Forgotten Corner of Hell.* Osprey Pub Co., 2002.

Warren, Alan. *Singapore.* Hambledon Press, 2003.

Wright, Derrick. *Tarawa—A Hell of a Way to Die.* Crowood Press, 2002.

Wright, Derrick. *The Battle for Iwo Jima.* Sutton, 2003.

Wright, Derrick. *Tarawa 1943; The Turning of the Tide.* Praeger Publishers, 2004.

The following books provide fascinating first-hand accounts by people who experienced the Pacific War, either as combatants or civilians:

Lewis, Jon E., ed. *Eye Witness to D Day: The Story of the Battle by Those Who Were There.* Carol and Graf, 1994.

Cook, Haruko Taya and Theodore F. Cook, *Japan At War: An Oral History.* New Press, Reprint edition, 1993.

Terkel, Studs. *The Good War.* Pantheon Books, 1984.

The following books provide or include interesting accounts of the Pacific War as a whole, although some may include highly detailed information. In these cases, use the Table of Contents or Index to find out more about a particular battle or aspect of the war:

Spector, Ronald H. *Eagle Against the Sun.* Free Press, 1991.

Lewis, Jonathan and Ben Steele. *Hell In The Pacific,* Macmillan Pub. Ltd., 2001.

Ian Dear and M.R.D. Foot, eds. *The Oxford Companion to World War II.* Oxford University Press, 2001.

Van Der Vat, Dan. *The Pacific Campaign,* Berlinn Limited, 2001.

Horner, David. *Inside the War Cabinet: Directing Australia's War Effort, 1939-1945.* Allen and Unwin, 1996.

RECOMMENDED VIDEOS

The following films, available on VHS or DVD, are set in the context of the Pacific War:

Empire of the Sun (1987)
Sands of Iwo Jima (1950)
The Bridge on the River Kwai (1957)
Tora! Tora! Tora! (1970)

The following are documentaries about the Pacific War:

Chronicles of World War II, with Walter Cronkite:
   Vol. 2: *The Pacific War Begins* and Vol. 7: *The Pacific Campaign* (1981), 20th Century Fox
Hell in the Pacific (2001), Carlton Visual Entertainment
V Is for Victory—America Goes to War—Guadalcanal and the Pacific Counterattack (1998), Accord Media UK
Battle Cry: Objective Burma—Operation Pacific (2003), Warner Home Videos

RECOMMENDED WEB SITES

www.combinedfleet.com/map.htm
View maps and summaries of naval engagements in the Pacific War.
www.historyplace.com
Click on the World War II tab for photographs of U.S. troops in the Pacific War, a timeline, and features on Pearl Harbor and African Americans in the war.
www.iwm.org.uk/
The web site for the Imperial War Museum in London.
www.nimitz-museum.org/
Web site for the U.S. National Museum of the Pacific War.
www.spartacus.schoolnet.co.uk/2WWpacific.htm
Contains a helpful summary of the Pacific War with many useful links along the way.

Note to parents and teachers
Every effort has been made by the publishers to ensure that these web sites are suitable for children; that they are of the highest educational value; and that they contain no inappropriate or offensive material. The nature of the Internet, however, makes it impossible to guarantee that the contents of these sites will not be altered. We strongly advise that a responsible adult supervises Internet access.

PLACES TO VISIT

The National Museum of the Pacific War is the only institution in the continental United States dedicated exclusively to telling the story of the Pacific Theater battles of World War II. It is located at:

The National Museum of the Pacific War, 340 East Main Street, Fredericksburg, Texas 78624.

Other important museums in the United States include:

The Naval Historical Center, Washington Naval Yard, Washington, D.C. 20374 (*www.history.navy.mil*)
The USS *Arizona* Visitor Center, Pearl Harbor Naval Base, Hawaii.

ABOUT THE AUTHOR

The author, Sean Sheehan, is a full-time writer who previously worked as a teacher in London and the Far East. While visiting sites and locations associated with World War II in Singapore and Malaysia, he began to research the history of World War II. He is also the author of *Germany and Japan Attack* and *World War II: The Alllied Victory*.

INDEX

Numbers in **bold** refer to captions to pictures or, where indicated, to maps.